OECD Reviews on Local Job Creation

Future-Proofing Adult Learning in Berlin, Germany

This document, as well as any data and map included herein, are without prejudice to the status of or sovereignty over any territory, to the delimitation of international frontiers and boundaries and to the name of any territory, city or area.

The statistical data for Israel are supplied by and under the responsibility of the relevant Israeli authorities. The use of such data by the OECD is without prejudice to the status of the Golan Heights, East Jerusalem and Israeli settlements in the West Bank under the terms of international law.

Please cite this publication as:
OECD (2022), *Future-Proofing Adult Learning in Berlin, Germany*, OECD Reviews on Local Job Creation, OECD Publishing, Paris, https://doi.org/10.1787/fdf38f60-en.

ISBN 978-92-64-33397-0 (print)
ISBN 978-92-64-37438-6 (pdf)

OECD Reviews on Local Job Creation
ISSN 2311-2328 (print)
ISSN 2311-2336 (online)

Photo credits: Cover © chrisinthai/Getty

Corrigenda to publications may be found on line at: www.oecd.org/about/publishing/corrigenda.htm.
© OECD 2022

The use of this work, whether digital or print, is governed by the Terms and Conditions to be found at https://www.oecd.org/termsandconditions.

Foreword

Two years into the COVID-19 pandemic, governments around the world are still managing the economic crisis caused by it. Lockdown and social-distancing measures aimed at protecting public health in Germany gave rise to an unprecedented economic shock, leading to a fall in GDP in Berlin that was three times higher than after the financial crisis of 2008. While Berlin's economy is slowly recovering and is projected to reach pre-crisis GDP levels in the first months of 2022, this OECD report still comes at a time of great uncertainty. New COVID-19 variants have driven additional and even larger waves of infections, again leading to extensive teleworking and a disruption of work processes in many sectors of the economy. While Berlin seems to have weathered the storm relatively well, with employment surpassing pre-pandemic levels, the pandemic has nonetheless brought several fault lines into the spotlight. The recovery has been unequal, with vulnerable segments of Berlin's labour force experiencing greater effects in terms of job and salary losses or underemployment.

The COVID-19 pandemic is not only causing economic uncertainty but is also accelerating the transformation of Berlin's labour market. Even before COVID-19, automation, digitalisation, job polarisation, and the emergence of non-standard forms of work, such as platform work, had been changing jobs and the demand for skills in Berlin. The pandemic has increased the pace of this transformation, with firms and workers adopting remote working, new technologies and digital services, further driving automation and digitalisation. The risks and benefits of the labour market transformation are uneven. The risks are particularly high for some groups in Berlin, such as low-skilled workers and migrants, who have lower levels of education on average and lower labour market attachment. As those groups make up a sizable proportion of the labour force in Berlin, designing tailored policy responses that help those at-risk workers navigate the changing labour market are essential.

This OECD report examines current and future opportunities and challenges that Berlin's labour market faces. It analyses Berlin's existing adult learning system and highlights options for making the system more effective and more closely aligned with local labour market needs, which would help address widespread skills mismatches and gaps. The report underlines the significance of adult learning and continuing education and training for Berlin's prosperity and its ability to manage the labour transformation effectively. In fact, adult learning is now more important than ever, with continuous learning and training part of a new normal for the labour force. This argument holds in particular for vulnerable groups and workers in jobs at risk of displacement. For these parts of Berlin's population, adult learning provides a gateway to re-train for positions in different occupations and sectors, gain new skills or refresh old ones, or upskill to move into better jobs.

This report is part of the series OECD Reviews on Local Job Creation within the Programme of Work of the OECD Local Employment and Economic Development (LEED) Programme. Created in 1982, the LEED Programme aims to contribute to the creation of more and better jobs for more productive and inclusive economies. It produces guidance to make the implementation of national policies more effective at the local level, and to stimulate innovative local practices that can be scaled up. The OECD LEED Directing Committee, which gathers governments of OECD member and non-member countries, oversees the work of the LEED Programme.

Acknowledgements

This report was prepared by the OECD Centre for Entrepreneurship, SMEs, Regions and Cities led by Lamia Kamal-Chaoui, Director. This work was conducted as part of the OECD's Local Economic and Employment Development (LEED) Programme with financial support from the JPMorgan Chase Foundation.

The report and underlying project were co-ordinated by Lukas Kleine-Rueschkamp under the supervision of Karen Maguire, Head of the Local Employment, Skills and Social Innovation (LESI) Division, OECD. Lukas Kleine-Rueschkamp and Lars Ludolph (both OECD) drafted the report and conducted the analysis. The report benefited from valuable contributions from Kristine Langenbucher, Head of Unit for Employment and Skills, LESI, OECD. Eric Gonnard and Tahsin Mehdi (both OECD) provided helpful statistical support. Pilar Philip and François Iglesias (both OECD) prepared the report for publication.

The OECD Secretariat expresses its gratitude to many stakeholders of the Berlin adult learning landscape. Special thanks are due to the Berlin Senate Department for Integration, Labour and Social Affairs and Integration and the Berlin Senate Department for Education, Youth and Families. In particular, Kirsten Bagusch-Sauermann and Dr. Ulrich Raiser supported the OECD throughout the project in facilitating contacts with employers, training providers, and social partners in Berlin. The OECD also thanks Julian Algner and Stefanie Dümmig (both IHK Berlin-Brandenburg), Anke Döring and Janine Fischer (both Bundesagentur für Arbeit), Anne von Oswald (Projektkontor für Bildung und Forschung), Angela Dovifat (Goldrausch eV), Manjiri Palicha (VHS Berlin-Mitte), Uwe Krzewina (VHS Neukoelln), Thomas Gill (Berliner Landeszentrale für politische Bildung), Anne Kjaer Bathel and Isabelle Köhncke (both REDI School of Digital Integration) and Frank Schröder (k.o.s GmbH) for extensive comments and exchanges with the OECD.

Special thanks are also extended to Hanka Boldemann, Executive Director Global Philanthropy at JPMorgan Chase Foundation.

Table of contents

Foreword 3

Acknowledgements 4

Acronyms and abbreviations 8

Executive summary 10

1 Assessment and recommendations 13
    Managing labour market uncertainty due to COVID-19 and the future of work 13
    What are the policy opportunities for Berlin to future-proof its adult learning system? 14

2 Berlin's labour market: Positive long-term trends, but socio-economic disparities persist 21
    Introduction 23
    Berlin has experienced a recent boom in the labour market 24
    Social divisions characterise Berlin's population and economy 32
    References 39

3 The impact of the future of work on Berlin's labour market 41
    Introduction 43
    How does automation affect Berlin's labour market? 43
    Changing skills needs in Berlin 53
    References 62
    Notes 64

4 Strengthening adult learning for inclusion and social mobility 65
    CET participation in Berlin: a national and international comparison 67
    Berlin's CET landscape: Funding and service delivery 75
    Increasing participation in CET among vulnerable population groups for a better labour market integration 91
    References 98

Tables

Table 3.1. Automation bottlenecks 45
Table 3.2. Automation bottleneck correspondence 45
Table 4.1. CET offered by companies of all sizes dropped sharply during COVID-19 73

Table 4.2. CET guidance in Berlin	80
Table 4.3. Different types of financial incentive schemes offered by the German federal government	82
Table 4.4. The generosity of educational leave laws across German federal states	84
Table 4.5. CET employers' networks in Berlin	90

Figures

Figure 2.1. The geography of Berlin	23
Figure 2.2. Berlin's unemployment rate dropped sharply between 2010 and 2019 relative to major metropolitan areas in the OECD	24
Figure 2.3. Berlin's unemployment rate remains the highest among Germany's federal states	25
Figure 2.4. Berlin's labour force participation rate is now on a par with other European metropolitan areas	26
Figure 2.5. Berlin's labour force participation rate is now close to the German average	27
Figure 2.6. New jobs in Berlin were created mostly in different service sectors	27
Figure 2.7. Berlin's labour productivity rose slowly since 2008	28
Figure 2.8. The total number of vacancies in Berlin increased between 2010 and 2019	29
Figure 2.9. Berlin's labour market tightened significantly between 2010 and 2019	30
Figure 2.10. Job vacancies in Berlin's service sector were on the rise before the COVID-19 pandemic	30
Figure 2.11. The share of companies struggling to fill vacancies increased across Germany over the past decade	31
Figure 2.12. Berlin's companies increasingly struggle to find suitable candidates	32
Figure 2.13. Education profile of Berlin's working-age population in national and international comparison	33
Figure 2.14. Berlin has one of the highest rates of early leavers from education and training in Germany	34
Figure 2.15. A large share of Berlin's young population is not in education and unemployed or inactive (NEET)	35
Figure 2.16. Migrants in Germany predominantly live in West German cities	36
Figure 2.17. The majority of migrants originate from outside the EU and are distributed unevenly across Berlin	36
Figure 2.18. The labour market attachment of migrants is relatively low in all of Berlin's boroughs	37
Figure 2.19. A relatively large share of Berlin's migrants fall into the low education category	38
Figure 3.1. Almost every second job in Berlin faces risks of automation	44
Figure 3.2. Automation risks are greater in the rest of Germany than in Berlin	46
Figure 3.3. Berlin has the largest share of employment in industries at low risk of automation in Germany	47
Figure 3.4. The majority of newly created jobs in Berlin are in high-skilled occupations with lower automation risks	48
Figure 3.5. Mean probability of automation	49
Figure 3.6. Job polarisation in Berlin is less pronounced than in most other OECD metropolitan areas	51
Figure 3.7. Employment risks due to the net-zero transition are small in Berlin	52
Figure 3.8. More than 40% of workers in Berlin are mismatched by level of qualification	54
Figure 3.9. Non-standard employment has been rising across OECD countries	56
Figure 3.10. More than a quarter of 16 to 64 year olds in Berlin have part-time work	57
Figure 3.11. Self-employment in Berlin has increased	58
Figure 3.12. Labour demand for advanced ICT skills has increased in Berlin during the pandemic	59
Figure 3.13. Labour demand for generic ICT skills remained unchanged during the pandemic	60
Figure 3.14. Almost everyone uses the internet regularly in OECD metropolitan areas	61
Figure 3.15. Only 45% of internet users in Berlin perform basic tasks online	62
Figure 4.1. Participation in education and training that excludes guided on-the-job training is low in Berlin compared to other OECD metropolitan areas	70
Figure 4.2. Participation in education and training that excludes guided on-the-job training is high in Berlin compared to other German federal states	70
Figure 4.3. Berlin lags behind other German federal states for work-related formal and non-formal CET participation	71
Figure 4.4. The share of Berlin's population participating in work-related formal and non-formal CET has remained constant over time	72
Figure 4.5. Small companies in Berlin rely heavily on self-studying methods	74
Figure 4.6. CET measures in Germany are mostly funded by individuals and companies	76
Figure 4.7. The total number of educational leave takers in Berlin is growing slowly over the years	85
Figure 4.8. Enterprises in Berlin declare financial support the main type of support needed to expand CET within the company	86
Figure 4.9. Employers in Berlin increasingly attach importance to digital skills training	88
Figure 4.10. VHS offers in Berlin are generous compared to other German federal states	91

| Figure 4.11. More than half of the courses offered by Berlin's VHS are language courses | 92 |
| Figure 4.12. Berlin's VHS do not currently offer counselling on labour market integration | 93 |

Boxes

Box 2.1. Why are employment rates among migrants often lower than that of native-born?	38
Box 3.1. Estimating the risk of automation across OECD countries and metropolitan areas	44
Box 3.2. Which industries have the highest risk of automation?	48
Box 3.3. Lancashire Digital Skills Partnership, UK	50
Box 3.4. Assessing employment risks due to the-zero transition	53
Box 3.5. Tools used by the Federal Employment Agency to analyse regional labour demand in Berlin	54
Box 3.6. Defining non-standard work	55
Box 3.7. Methodology to calculate ICT skill demand based on online job postings	60
Box 4.1. Differences between formal, informal and non-formal education and their measurement in different German data sources	67
Box 4.2. The link between population density and informal learning	69
Box 4.3. The new law on "adult learning in Berlin"	78
Box 4.4. Combining economic and societal objectives in adult learning in London, UK	79
Box 4.5. The Waff training account – education and training options for own-account workers in Vienna, Austria	83
Box 4.6. Germany has recently introduced two new laws that strengthen financial support for training and education measures offered by SMEs	87
Box 4.7. Supporting growth and social investments in SMEs through skill development in Vantaa, Finland	89
Box 4.8. Labour market counselling for migrants at the VHS Wiesbaden, Hessen	93
Box 4.9. Berlin's "alpha label" to facilitate basic education and social inclusion	95
Box 4.10. Teaching migrants coding and programming: The ReDI School of digital integration	96
Box 4.11. Combining language and vocational training for migrants – local initiatives in Sweden	96

Acronyms and abbreviations

AEB	Adult education budget
AI	Artificial intelligence
ALMPs	Active labour market policies
BA	Federal Employment Agency (Bundesagentur für Arbeit)
BAMF	Federal Office for Migration and Refugees (Bundesamt für Migration und Flüchtlinge)
BBB	Berlin guidance on education and profession network (Berliner Beratung zu Bildung und Beruf)
BDA	Confederation of German Employers' Associations (Bundesvereinigung der Deutschen Arbeitgeberverbände)
BiZeitG	Berlin educational leave law (Berliner Bildungszeitgesetz)
BMAS	German Federal Ministry of Labour and Social Affairs (Bundesministerium für Arbeit und Soziales)
BMBF	Federal Ministry of Education and Research (Bundesministerium für Bildung und Forschung)
CET	Continuing education and training
DCMS	UK Department for Digital, Culture, Media and Sport
DIE	German Institute for Adult Education (Deutsches Institut für Erwachsenenbildung)
ERDF	European Regional Development Fund
ESCO	European skills, competences, qualifications and occupations taxonomy
ESF	European Social Fund
EU-LFS	European Labour Force Survey
GBZ	Centre for Basic Education (Grund-Bildungs-Zentrum)
GDP	Gross domestic product
GLA	Greater London Authority
GOTJ	Guided on-the-job training
IAB	Institute for Employment Research (Institut für Arbeitsmarkt- und Berufsforschung)
ICT	Information and communication technology
IHK	Chamber of Commerce and Industry (Industrie- und Handelskammer)
ISCED	International standard classification of education

ISCO	International standard classification of occupations
ISIC	Industrial classification of all economic activities
IVET	Initial vocational education and training
LBBiE	Lifelong vocational guidance for adults in employment (Lebensbegleitende Berufsberatung im Erwerbsleben).
LDSP	Lancashire Digital Skills Partnership
LEP	Lancashire Enterprise Partnership's skills and employment hub
LPBB	Berlin Agency for Civic Education (Landeszentrale für Politische Bildung Berlin)
MoBiBe	Mobile guidance on education and employment for refugees (Mobile Beratung zu Bildung und Beruf für geflüchtete Menschen)
NACE	Statistical classification of economic activities in the European Community
NEET	Youth not in employment, education, or training
NGO	Non-governmental organisation
NSW	Non-standard work
NUTS	Nomenclature of territorial units for statistics
NWS	National skills strategy (Nationale Weiterbildungsstrategie)
O*NET	Occupational information network
PES	Public employment services
PIAAC	Programme for the international assessment of adult competencies
SBS	Structural business statistics
SenBJF	Senate Department for Education, Youth and Family (Senatsverwaltung für Bildung, Jugend und Familie)
SenGPG	Senate Department for Health, Care and Equality (Senatsverwaltung für Gesundheit, Pflege und Gleichstellung)
SenIAS	Senate Department for Integration, Labour and Social Affairs (Senatsverwaltung für Integration, Arbeit und Soziales)
SMEs	Small and medium-sized enterprises
VHS	Adult education centres (Volkshochschulen)
WDB	CET database Berlin (Berliner Weiterbildungsdatenbank)

Executive summary

Berlin is Germany's capital, its biggest city with a population of almost 3 650 000 and one of its 16 federal states. While the city has a labour force of more than 2 million, due to Germany's decentralised economy it is neither Germany's financial capital nor the city with the most headquarters of large enterprises. Berlin's population has grown by more than 8% since 2000. It is one of the most diverse across Germany, with around one-third of its residents having a migration background.

Over the past decade, Berlin's labour market has significantly tightened. The unemployment rate has been falling from 13% in 2010 to 5.5% in 2019. Following a decade of rapid employment growth driven by the service sector, Berlin's labour market has now entered a new period. Recruitment of suitably qualified workers is becoming increasingly difficult for employers. Since 2010, the number of job vacancies has almost tripled and reached around 115 000 jobs in 2019. Ultimately, this development will put upward pressure on wages in sectors that experience shortages in labour supply and could reduce productivity growth of firms that cannot fill vacancies.

The tightening of Berlin's labour market raises the importance of the local adult learning system for two reasons. First, the system will need to increase the supply of qualified workers that can meet the skills needs of Berlin employers. Second, as wages are likely to rise disproportionally in high-skill sectors, there is a risk of aggravated social divisions if low and medium-educated workers are not trained and upskilled to remain attractive to local employers.

While the pandemic has been the focus of much of the policy discourse in the past two years, Berlin had already faced several labour market challenges that require an effective adult learning system. The crisis has put the spotlight on these challenges. Educational attainment in Berlin has been rising but it remains below that of many other OECD metropolitan areas. Additionally, many inhabitants of Berlin are not making optimal use of their skills. Around 41% of workers are mismatched by qualification, the second highest degree of mismatch among 13 major OECD metropolitan areas. Such skills mismatches and gaps affect not only workers, but also have a negative impact on employers and thus local economic growth. Employers are struggling to fill vacancies with suitable staff, particularly in services such as health, social services and education.

The pandemic also compounds labour market trends that risk exacerbating socio-economic inequality in Berlin. As a catalyst for technological change, COVID-19 accelerates megatrends such as digitalisation and the automation of production processes. Already before the pandemic, Berlin faced higher automation risks than many other OECD metropolitan areas. Almost half of all workers in Berlin (47%) could be directly affected by automation, compared to less than 30% in cities such as Oslo or London. Those workers need tailored support via skills development and adult learning before they become unemployed.

The challenges for Berlin's labour market call for greater efforts aimed at enhancing and future-proofing the adult learning and continuous education system in Berlin. Employers play a vital role in offering training, learning and skills development opportunities in Germany. However, employers in Berlin do not invest enough into training and learning for their employees. Only 14% of the labour force participated in work-related training in Berlin in 2019, the lowest participation rate among all German states.

Financial resources and capacity constraints are major obstacles for most firms in Berlin to provide training. However, they affect SMEs, microenterprises and own-account workers the most. Only 28% of enterprises with less than 10 employees in Berlin offer education and training opportunities, compared to 76% of larger enterprises with more than 250 employees. The fact that Berlin has the highest share of self-employed (13.5%) in Germany exacerbates these constraints. Additionally, own-account workers without any employees make up 74% of all self-employed in Berlin compared to 54% nationally, which further limits participation and investment in adult learning.

Berlin recognises the importance of skills and a functioning adult learning system to support skills development and the local labour market. In 2021, Berlin's first Adult Education Act came into force. Furthermore, during the pandemic the exchange between the responsible ministries in Berlin and other key stakeholders such as employer federations, social partners and learning providers has also intensified. Nonetheless, participation in adult learning and continuous education remains low in Berlin compared to other German states and is only half that of the leading OECD metropolitan areas. If Berlin were to catch-up with cities like Zurich, Helsinki or Stockholm, nearly half a million more adults would need to participate in training every year. Additionally, general adult learning and training for the labour market are separately defined and managed, even though a better integration could reap significant benefits.

Addressing the barriers to accessing adult learning, supported by a long-term comprehensive skills and adult learning strategy, is within the scope of public action in Berlin. To future-proof the adult learning system, Berlin could build on the following policy recommendations laid out in this OECD report:

Develop a long-term strategy for adult learning in Berlin

- **Develop a new master plan for skills development and adult education:** The rapid labour market transformation requires a comprehensive strategy with a clear vision and objectives for the future of Berlin's labour market and economy. Creating a new advisory board that includes workers, social partners and employers could help inform and steer the strategic direction of skills development policies and ensure that it aligns with local skills needs.
- **Encourage a culture of life-long learning:** Creating stronger links between general adult learning and work-related continuing education and training could help enhance learners' willingness to stay involved in Berlin's adult learning system. Capitalising on Berlin's general adult education provision could support transversal skills that matter for a work-related context and foster "learning to learn".

Provide adult learning to all individuals and tailor it to the needs of vulnerable groups

- **Ensure learning and retraining opportunities reach workers most at risk of labour market transformation:** This could include an expansion of short, modular courses and online training as a complement to traditional learning modules. Introducing education and training instruments that target own-account workers and account for their greater need for flexibility could enhance access to training and participation.
- **Expand learning opportunities for both basic as well as digital skills:** Opportunities could include embedding digital skills training in adult learning programmes and expanding the Berlin *Alphabetisierungskampagne* ("literacy campaign") and the work of the *Grundbildungszentrum Berlin* ("Berlin Centre for Basic Education"). Furthermore, Berlin could scale up social economy programmes that offer targeted support for youth who leave school early or lack basic skills.
- **Adapt the adult learning offer for migrants to their specific needs:** A closer integration of education, labour market and career guidance services into Berlin's *Volkshochschulen* ("Adult Education Centres") could turn them into "one-stop-shops" for the economic and societal integration of migrants. Berlin could also scale up learning and training offers to migrants in areas that do not require German language proficiency, such as the IT sector.

Encourage employer involvement in adult learning and training

- **Foster demand-led training and labour market information:** Increasing employer representation in the planning of skills policies could create a better alignment with labour market needs. Setting up regular surveys of enterprises in Berlin to collect comprehensive data on skills challenges in recruitment and with the existing workforce could help inform the design of effective training programmes.

- **Strengthen workplace training and tailor support to the needs of SMEs:** Berlin could aim to establish peer-learning platforms that spread good workplace practices and share resources for training among both small and large firms. Additionally, Berlin could raise awareness of the value of training and learning among SMEs, by employing dedicated project account managers that contact SMEs proactively, help them develop a joint skills needs assessment, and identify suitable training programmes.

1 Assessment and recommendations

Managing labour market uncertainty due to COVID-19 and the future of work

Berlin is Germany's capital and largest city with a population of almost 3 650 000. As one of 16 federal states in Germany, Berlin has greater autonomy in various policy areas than most OECD cities, notably in culture, primary, secondary and tertiary education as well as media. Berlin has a labour force of more than 2 million but, due to Germany's decentralised economy, it is neither the country's financial capital nor the city with the most headquarters of large enterprises. The metropolitan area of Berlin, which also includes its commuting zones in the neighbouring state of Brandenburg, accounts for 6.4% of the national population but only 5.8% of national gross domestic product (GDP). In Germany, Berlin is one of the fastest growing and most diverse cities. Its population has grown by more than 8% since 2000 and around one-third of its residents have a migration background.

This OECD report comes at a time of great change that will continue to transform Berlin's economy and labour market. The economy is still affected by the COVID-19 pandemic. While it caused an economic contraction in the first wave, it continues to create uncertainty for Berlin's economy. Just as the labour market in Berlin recovered from the shock caused by confinement and social distancing measures, new waves and COVID-19 variants give again rise for concern. While Berlin has weathered the storm relatively well, with unemployment falling even during the pandemic, underemployment has grown as many firms struggle financially and some workers remain on short-time work schemes.

Before the onset of the COVID-19 outbreak, Berlin had enjoyed two decades of rising employment and economic growth. Between 2000 and 2019, total employment in Berlin grew at an annual rate of almost 1.3%, compared to 0.7% in Germany and 0.6% in the European Union, creating almost 450 000 new jobs. During this period, Berlin also experienced gains in its labour productivity, which helped to reduce the gap with other major OECD metropolitan areas. Nonetheless, labour productivity remains 40 to 50% below that of OECD metropolitan areas such as Amsterdam, Stockholm, Oslo or Paris. While the uncertainty and economic effects of the COVID-19 pandemic might put some of the gains in productivity and employment that Berlin made over the past decade at risk, its labour market appears to be entering a new phase.

Berlin's labour market is increasingly tightening, as labour supply struggles to keep up with rising labour demand. Recruitment of suitably qualified workers is becoming increasingly difficult for employers. Since 2010, the number of job vacancies has almost tripled and reached around 115 000 jobs in 2019. Over the same period, the unemployment rate fell from 13% to 5.5%. As a result, the pool of readily available workers has declined. In 2010, approximately nine unemployed workers were available for each open position but this ratio dropped to almost one in 2019. More than 40% of firms in Berlin and neighbouring Brandenburg reported difficulties in finding a suitable candidate for a vacancy in 2019, an increase of 10 percentage points since 2010. Besides a lack of available workers, more than a quarter of firms cite a lack of sufficient professional qualifications as a major obstacle in recruitment, indicating the skills gaps that hold back their businesses and, ultimately, economic and productivity growth in Berlin.

The pandemic has not only led to a widespread adoption of teleworking but has also accelerated megatrends that continue to transform Berlin's labour market and could accelerate skills gaps. Even before the pandemic, Berlin faced a number of profound challenges as digitalisation and automation changed the types of jobs and skills needed in the labour market. As in previous economic crises, COVID-19 has accelerated the adoption of new technologies that will further speed up the transformation of Berlin's labour market. Due to automation, almost every second job in Berlin could be affected, and either see a significant change to its requirements in terms of tasks and skills (32%) or could disappear entirely (14%). Supporting those workers before they become unemployed requires tailored adult learning offers that enable them to upskill or retrain.

Already before the pandemic, Berlin faced significant challenges in terms of skills gaps and mismatches. Educational attainment in Berlin has been rising but it remains below that of many other OECD metropolitan areas. Additionally, many inhabitants of Berlin are not making optimal use of their skills, and work in jobs that do not match their qualifications. Around 41% of workers are mismatched by qualification, the second highest degree of mismatch among 13 major OECD metropolitan areas. Such skills mismatches and gaps reduce worker productivity and local economic growth, as firms struggle to fill vacancies with suitable staff. Besides skills mismatches among the employed, Berlin also faces challenges in preparing youth for the labour market. Around 14% of individuals aged 18 to 24 leave education without a degree, three percentage points above the German average, heightening the risk that they do not have the necessary skills to find employment.

The adult learning system in Berlin plays an important role in how the city can manage the labour market transformation. Effective alignment of labour market needs with training and learning offers can help alleviate skills gaps that many employers in Berlin experience. A strong adult learning system with tailored training and learning opportunities helps workers to take up new and emerging opportunities more readily. It also provides an essential tool for raising social mobility, especially among low-skilled individuals and youth. Furthermore, it fosters the integration of migrants and refugees, which is particularly important in Berlin because a third of its population has a migration background.

What are the policy opportunities for Berlin to future-proof its adult learning system?

This OECD report has been developed following extensive consultations with stakeholders across Berlin, including the Senate Department for Integration, Labour and Social Affairs and the Senate Department for Education, Youth and Families. Additionally, the OECD consulted with the regional branch of the Federal Employment Agency, the Chamber of Industry and Commerce, as well as a large range of adult learning and continuous education providers. As Berlin aims to enhance its adult learning system, the following recommendations could be considered.

Develop a long-term strategy for adult learning in Berlin

Berlin has made important progress in recognising the importance of adult learning and continuous education, and learners benefit from a diverse landscape of learning opportunities. The new *Erwachsenenbildungsgesetz* ("Law on Adult Learning") in Berlin aims to give new impetus to the expansion of adult learning opportunities and the provision of necessary support for potential learners. A combination of a wide range of adult learning providers, business associations and direct programmes of the city administration offer diverse and manifold training and learning programmes. Nonetheless, a number of weaknesses undermine the efficacy of Berlin's adult learning system.

While adult learning and continuous education are more important than ever before, Berlin currently lacks a comprehensive long-term plan that lays out a clear and comprehensive skills

strategy for Berlin. Berlin's labour market is changing rapidly and many promising skills development initiatives exist under the umbrella of both the Berlin Senate and the German federal government. However, these are currently fragmented. A broader vision for the city's skills strategy, including strategic responses to long-term labour market megatrends, would counter skills gaps and mismatches and support Berlin's citizens to re- and upskill throughout their working lives.

In designing a long-term skills and adult learning strategy, Berlin could draw upon insights of this OECD report and build upon ideas that had been previously identified by relevant local stakeholders. Berlin's *Masterplan Qualifizierung* ("Master Plan Qualification"), published in 2011, envisioned a long-term skills strategy. It was developed by the Senate Department for Integration, Labour and Social Affairs in co-operation with the biggest adult learning actors in Berlin. Revitalising the coalition behind that plan and working together with other adult learning providers could help Berlin address the major challenges its adult learning and continuous education system will face.

Currently, general adult learning as well as labour market related training and learning are separately defined and managed. While the Senate Department for Integration, Labour and Social Affairs is responsible for vocational education and labour market policies, responsibilities for more general adult education and lifelong learning lie within the Senate Department for Education, Youth and Families. This strict separation of the adult learning system risks forgoing the benefits of links and synergies that exist between those two strands. For example, the bulk of German language classes falls under general adult education under the Senate Department for Education, Youth and Families, but has clear implications for migrant labour market opportunities in Berlin. While the Berlin Adult Learning Law provides positive momentum for general adult education, the law exemplifies the strong divide between general adult education and labour market specific training in Berlin. Its advisory board is heavily skewed towards general adult education and lacks representation from enterprises, which could further widen the gap between general adult education and labour market training.

Berlin's diverse adult learning landscape has many providers that offer a wide range of learning programmes, but they are difficult to navigate for learners and workers. While the system offers learners a broad set of choices, its fragmented structure can make it difficult for potential interested learners or employers to identify programmes that best fit their needs. Through two websites, Berlin and the regional branch of the federal employment agency aim to provide an overview of existing adult learning programmes. Building on these efforts, as well as helping employers to navigate and take advantage of those programmes, could facilitate the search of both individuals as well as employers of suitable programmes that match their specific needs, skills and qualification. Jointly with an integrated long-term skills strategy, such a database might also help alleviate confusion around "who offers what" in the Berlin adult learning landscape.

Recommendations for developing a long-term strategy for adult learning in Berlin

Create a new master plan or long-term strategy for skills development and adult education

- *Develop a clear, comprehensive and long-term skills strategy for Berlin.* The rapid transformation of the labour market requires a comprehensive and integrated approach that lays out a clear vision and objectives for the future of Berlin's labour market and economy. The strategy should entail the definition of short- and long-term goals, and build on timely data as well as forecasting analysis to anticipate future changes to skills needs. Examples to follow could include the skills strategy in London that defines clear economic and social indicators and objectives.
- *Support long-term objectives with the creation of a diverse advisory board that helps inform and steer the strategic direction of skills development policies in Berlin.* Bringing together employees, political decision makers, social partners, adult learning providers and local employers could help Berlin to design and follow a skills strategy that aligns with local labour market needs and simultaneously pursues social objectives such as social mobility, lifelong learning and support of vulnerable groups.
- *Examine opportunities for integrating job-related training and general adult learning policies.* The current system has two separate strands, one for general adult education as well as lifelong learning and another strand for vocational as well as job-related training. While these strands may pursue different objectives, they also offer clear synergies in areas such as language training or digital skills.

Foster quality information and advice about careers and jobs in Berlin

- *Leverage the promising local database Weiterbildungsdatenbank Berlin ("continuous education database") to facilitate participation in learning and training offers.* To make the most of the comprehensive overview of continuous education and training (CET) offers in Berlin via the Weiterbildungsdatenbank, policy makers in Berlin could look at a number of options. First, increasing the visibility of the database and raising awareness among firms and potential learners is essential. Second, many learners might be deterred from taking advantage of existing offers due to time or financial constraints. To boost CET uptake, it would be helpful to link the entries in the database with detailed information on support measures such as financial incentives, which is already the case, as well as to link directly to the required documents to obtain such support.
- *Ensure Berlin can leverage timely labour market data and information on skills needs to shape adult learning decisions and priorities.* This would include regular information on employer labour market needs in terms of skills and qualifications, their challenges in using existing learning offers, improved access to consistent data on adult learning participation, learner progress, learner subsequent employment outcomes, and outcomes for individual local training providers.

Encourage a culture of life-long learning

- *Use public outreach and existing adult learning provision to foster awareness of the benefits of lifelong learning.* As younger generations are likely to need training and learning throughout their careers, establishing a strong culture of lifelong learning is vital. Here, the goal should be "learning to learn". Greater awareness of both the need for learning and its benefits are a prerequisite for encouraging individuals to engage in CET and general adult learning. Creating stronger links between different adult learning courses on the one hand, and general adult

learning and work-related CET on the other, could help enhance learner willingness to stay involved in Berlin's adult learning system.
- *Capitalise on Berlin's general adult education provision to foster transversal skills.* Berlin's general adult education can impart valuable competences that also matter for a work-related context. By strengthening transversal skills such as digital literacy, language competence, learning competence and basic literacy, the general adult learning provision can support work-related adult learning and training, and equip individuals with the toolkit to acquire other, more specific occupational skills.

Provide adult learning to all individuals and tailor it to the needs of vulnerable groups

The primary objective of adult and continuous education is to offer opportunities for retraining and upskilling. The groups that stand to benefit the most from such opportunities consist mainly of individuals who face heightened risks in the labour market. They include low-skilled workers whose jobs have a greater likelihood of being automated or markedly changed by automation. Other vulnerable groups consist of young people who enter the labour market or migrants that might not have the right skills demanded in the local economy or struggle with the recognition of their foreign qualifications.

Berlin could reap significant benefits from better integrating its migrant population into its continuous education system and ultimately its labour market. Around 33% of Berlin's working-age population has a migrant background, i.e. has no German citizenship or at least one parent does not hold German citizenship by birth. Berlin is home to many recent refugees who arrived over the last few years. On average, these groups record lower employment and educational attainment outcomes than the general population in Berlin. Making sure that adult learning and continuous education directly fosters the social and economic integration of migrants would generate significant benefits.

A better integration of general adult education offered primarily by *Volkshochschulen (VHS)* ("adult education centres") into the general continuous education and training system could encourage the economic integration of migrants. The demand for German language courses is very high, as newly arrived migrants aim to acquire the necessary language skills to participate economically. However, language courses alone do not suffice and becoming proficient requires time. Therefore, a stronger emphasis on combining language courses with work-related training could not only provide an attractive option to potential learners, but also equip them with the necessary vocational experience to thrive in Berlin's labour market. Systematically scaling up and institutionalising promising examples of existing efforts (e.g. REDI School as well as initiatives by VHS) could enhance the integration, skills development and economic mobility of migrants.

Despite many learning opportunities, low participation in learning and training courses holds back the adult learning system in Berlin. In an OECD comparison, participation in formal and non-formal education and training in Berlin is only half that of the leading OECD metropolitan areas. Within Germany, work-related continuous education and training is significantly below the levels of other German states. To raise participation among all types of employees, Berlin could seek to raise awareness of the local continuous education and training offer and its benefits. In particular, Berlin could expand the scope of programmes that target all workers in need, especially those who could be affected by automation. Given the accelerating change of the labour market, skills development and adult learning will need to increasingly serve not only the long-term unemployed and those facing barriers to the labour market, but also workers affected by labour market disruptions and technological change before they become unemployed.

Two important challenges for Berlin's labour market are the need to equip its workforce with both basic as well as digital skills. A significant share of the population lacks basic competencies in terms of literacy and numeracy, exacerbated by the fact that 14% of individuals aged 18 to 24 leave education without a degree, more than three percentage points above the German average. Such competencies are the necessary foundation for succeeding in the labour market. Furthermore, without adequate basic skills, it becomes extremely difficult to upskill and re-train as the skills needs of the economy change. This is particularly important for digital skills whose relevance is rising rapidly as firms adopt more and new technologies.

Recommendations for providing adult learning to all individuals and tailoring it to the needs of vulnerable groups

Ensure learning and retraining opportunities reach workers most at risk of labour market transformation

- *Strengthen foresight analytics to identify individuals at risk from emerging labour market transformations and raise awareness of the benefits of skills development.* Tailor services to the specific needs of individuals who face heightened risk from automation, digitalisation or the green transition. Strengthen career guidance that helps establish pathways into other jobs or sectors and boosts awareness of the benefits of adult training opportunities.

- *Work with adult learning providers to establish modular learning offers that enable easily accessible upskilling and re-training opportunities for all adults.* While Berlin already offers relatively generous work leave for learning and training, the rollout of more flexible and especially short, modular courses could encourage stronger uptake of those opportunities. It would enable workers to better balance adult learning participation with work or family responsibilities.

- *Introduce education and training instruments that target own-account workers.* Own-account workers, i.e. self-employed without any employees, constitute a much larger share of Berlin's labour force than in other German regions. Due to legal, financial and time constraints, their participation in continuous education and training (CET) is low. To increase CET participation among own-account workers, Berlin could follow a model similar to Vienna's Waff Training Account. The Waff Training Account explicitly includes own-account workers and accounts for their needs of great flexibility. It covers 80 percent of the total training costs up to a maximum of EUR 2 000 for business-relevant education and training, including digital skills. To facilitate use and increase take-up, CET applications can be submitted online before the training course begins or up until four weeks after the start date of the course.

Expand learning opportunities of both basic as well as digital skills

- *Strengthen efforts to reach individuals that lack basic skills.* Sufficient numeracy and literacy are not only the foundation for most jobs, but are a prerequisite for further learning. Thus, extending efforts such as the literacy campaign (*Alphabetisierungskampagne*) that try to offer on-the-ground support for people without basic skills could foster social and economic integration. To this end, the *Grundbildungszentrum Berlin* ("Berlin Centre for Basic Education"), funded by the Senate Department for Education, Youth and Families, is a promising institution. Its novel "alpha label" programme assigns quality labels to institutions that offer their services in an easily accessible way for adults with low literacy. Its use could be expanded across Berlin more widely.

- *Embed digital skills training in adult learning programmes.* Digital skills have become ever more relevant. Making sure that adult learning provision fosters the acquisition of digital skills, both basic as well as more advanced ICT skills, puts learners in a stronger position to find job opportunities or engage in learning more effectively.

Adapt the adult learning offer for migrants to their specific needs

- *Leverage participation in German language courses to provide career counselling and equip migrants with necessary vocational skills.* Combining language courses with direct work-related training offers significant synergies for preparing migrants for the labour market and could reduce the time they need for finding a job. In a first step, Berlin's Volkshochschulen (VHS) ("adult education centres") could offer career, education and labour market counselling to migrants and refugees, similar to the Volkshochschule Wiesbaden in Hessen, Germany. The VHS Wiesbaden institutionalised the approach taken by Berlin's Mobile Beratung zu Bildung und Beruf für geflüchtete Menschen (MoBiBe, "mobile counselling on education and careers for refugees"), a mobile counselling unit introduced by the Senate Department for Integration, Labour and Social Affairs in response to the 2015/2016 arrival of a large number of asylum seekers. In a second step, Berlin's VHS could expand the scope of existing offers that combine language training with vocational education, following international best-practice examples.

- *Scale up learning and training offers in areas that do not require German proficiency by building on successful social economy initiatives.* By offering training for in-demand sectors where English is the working language, or jobs in the IT sector where language skills are less relevant, migrants could gain early access to jobs without a lengthy period of acquiring German proficiency. To this end, Berlin could build on existing learning providers in its social economy such as the REDI School. The REDI School has developed a successful model that trains refugees in programming and coding and then cooperates with the private sector to place their graduates in Berlin's IT sector.

Strengthen the support for employers and bring employers on board to foster investments in adult learning and workplace training

Employers remain the main provider of continuous education and training (CET) in Berlin. The COVID-19 crisis has however shown that financial resources are scarce in times of recession. Almost three-quarters of employers in Berlin cite a lack of financial resources as an obstacle to expanding continuous education and training in their company. Other notable impediments include easy access to information on CET offers, CET counselling, and CET planning support.

The challenges employers face with respect to CET are even more pronounced for SMEs. SMEs and very small companies in particular tend to underinvest in CET due to a lack of resources, insufficient investment incentives and much lower capacity to offer internal training or learning opportunities. In Berlin, the share of very small businesses among SMEs and the share of self-employed individuals is higher than in other German regions. For them, tailored CET offers, better information on existing programmes and easier use of those programmes are especially important.

Aligning the adult learning and CET system with the skills needs of employers is essential for managing the transformation of the labour market efficiently and inclusively. This requires frequent and systematic exchange between employers and policy makers on the one hand, and employers and adult learning providers on the other hand. A crucial step would consist of better employer representation and involvement in the planning of skills needs and the new strategy. Since the onset of the COVID-19 pandemic, the Berlin Senate Department for Integration, Labour and Social Affairs has held regular meetings with relevant stakeholders, including employers, on skills and labour market issues. Institutionalising such exchanges and setting up dedicated business advisory groups on skills development could be a next step.

Recommendations for encouraging employer involvement in adult learning and training

Foster demand-led training and labour market information

- *Set-up regular surveys of enterprises in Berlin.* The survey could collect comprehensive data and information on skills challenges that employers report both within their existing workforces and when recruiting. Data collected could include the levels and nature of investment in training and development as well as the relationship between skills challenges, training activity and business strategy. Building upon and supporting the expansion of surveys by the *Industrie- und Handelskammer* ("Chamber of Industry and Commerce") or the *Institut für Arbeitsmarkt- und Berufsforschung* ("Institute for Employment Research") could yield such valuable information in a more frequent manner.

- *Increase employer representation in the planning of skills policies.* Since the COVID-19 pandemic, the Berlin Senate Chambers have organised regular meetings with business associations to discuss adult learning and labour market issues. Going forward, institutionalising such exchanges could ensure closer collaboration with the private sector. One option could be to set up a skills business advisory group that represents enterprises of different sizes and from different sectors and offers guidance to political decision makers. Furthermore, stronger collaboration and exchange of information between training providers and local firms could help shape CET programmes according to local needs and incentivise firms to make use of such training opportunities.

Strengthen workplace training and tailor support to the needs of SMEs

- *Establish peer-learning platforms that spread good workplace practices and share resources for training among firms in Berlin.* Such platforms could facilitate knowledge sharing of successful management practices, internal skills development strategies, and uptake of new technologies or other innovations. To this end, Berlin could support the newly-founded CET employer networks. These networks are funded by the federal government and bring together local companies to exchange on skill needs and training opportunities. To develop networks further and beyond the initial funding period, Berlin could aim to engage large companies in such networks. These large companies could then be encouraged to open their training courses and workshops outside of regular operating hours and, with their expertise, offer advanced training on the new machines and technologies for employees of SMEs.

- *Introduce new support measures for training in SMEs that go beyond financial incentives to raise awareness of the value of training and learning.* Ample funding opportunities for training and education in SMEs exist on the federal level, with the new *Qualifizierungschancengesetz* ("Skills Development Opportunities Act") and the *Arbeit-von-morgen-Gesetz* ("Work of Tomorrow Act") covering up to 100% of direct and indirect costs incurred by SMEs. However, awareness and take-up of these opportunities remain low among SMEs. Faced with similar problems, other cities across the OECD have started to acknowledge the need to go beyond financial incentives. For example, Berlin could pursue an approach similar to the city of Vantaa, Finland, where project account managers employed by the city are assigned to SMEs to contact SMEs proactively. Following a joint skills needs assessment, suitable training programmes are then suggested to SMEs and their employees.

2 Berlin's labour market: Positive long-term trends, but socio-economic disparities persist

This chapter describes Berlin's labour market and the socio-economic profile of its population. The first part characterises both the demand and the supply side of its labour market, with a particular focus on long-term trends in key indicators, such as changes in the demand for specific occupations, the local unemployment rate and labour force participation. The second part then focusses on the educational profile of Berlin's population. Throughout the chapter, cities from across the OECD and the other German federal states serve as benchmarks to put Berlin into perspective.

In Brief

After a long period of rapid employment growth driven by the service sector, Berlin's labour market is now tightening

- **Berlin's headline labour market indicators have improved steadily over the past decade.** Berlin's unemployment dropped from 13.0% in 2010 to 5.5% in 2019. Labour force participation increased from 76.0% in 2010 to 79.2% in 2019. Both labour market indicators are now on a par with other OECD capital cities. The simultaneous decline in Berlin's unemployment rate and the rise in its economic activity rate within the same age group of 15 to 64 year olds show that the positive labour market trends were indeed the result of local employment growth.

- **Employment growth in Berlin has been driven almost exclusively by the service sector.** Between 2000 and 2019, total employment in Berlin grew by an annual rate of almost 1.3%, compared to 0.7% in Germany and 0.6% in the European Union. This is equivalent to the creation of almost 450 000 new jobs in Berlin since 2000. Trade, transport, accommodation and food services (annual growth of 2.4%) and financial, insurance, real estate and business activities (annual growth of 1.6%) recorded the fastest employment growth. In contrast, employment in industrial jobs or construction fell by 37 000 and 22 000, respectively.

- **Berlin's labour productivity remains subpar compared to other OCED cities.** Since the financial crisis, Berlin has had low labour productivity growth compared to other OECD metropolitan areas. While many OECD cities recorded an increase in labour productivity of more than 10% between 2008 and 2018, labour productivity only grew by 6% in Berlin. Since labour productivity was relatively low before the financial crisis, the gap in gross value added per worker between Berlin and other OECD cities remains large.

- **The labour market in Berlin has tightened significantly and employers increasingly struggle to find suitable candidates to fill vacancies.** The ratio of unemployed per job vacancy dropped from approximately nine in 2010 to slightly above one in 2019 before rising again to two in 2020, the first year of the COVID-19 pandemic. As a result, Berlin's companies increasingly mention an insufficient number of applicants and an insufficient professional qualification of candidates as the main reasons why they struggle to fill job vacancies.

- **The relatively high share of tertiary educated in Berlin hides social disparities.** In 2020, 42% of Berlin's 25 to 64 year old population had attained tertiary education and are therefore considered highly educated, a share higher than in other German regions and only slightly below that of other major cities across the OECD. However, education indicators for the low educated paint a different picture. For example, the share of 18 to 24 year olds who are not currently in education and unemployed or inactive (NEET) stood at 10.2% in 2019, well above the German average of 7.7%.

- **The labour market attachment of Berlin's population with a migration background is low across all of Berlin's boroughs.** Migrants are mostly settled in Berlin's former Western parts, where the share of the population with a migration background reaches up to 54% (Berlin-Mitte). Seventy-two percent of those of working age with a migration background were economically active in 2019, compared to 83% among Germans without a migration background. Similarly, the unemployment rate among Germans without a migration background stood at 4% in Berlin, compared to 9% among those with a migration background.

Introduction

Berlin is the largest German city, one of 16 German federal states and the capital of Germany. In 2019, Berlin was home to 3 644 830 inhabitants, making it the biggest German city and metropolitan area. The city of Berlin is, next to Hamburg and Bremen, the only city-state of Germany. Geographically, Berlin is located approximately 70 kilometres west of the Polish border. It is surrounded by the significantly less densely populated federal state of Brandenburg (Figure 2.1, Panel A). Parts of Brandenburg, most note-worthy its capital Potsdam (178 000 inhabitants in 2019), fall into Berlin's commuting zone. Berlin is divided into 12 boroughs, which are administrative units with no autonomous competences (Figure 2.1, Panel B).

Figure 2.1. The geography of Berlin

Berlin's geographical position in Germany (Panel A) and the 12 boroughs of Berlin (Panel B)

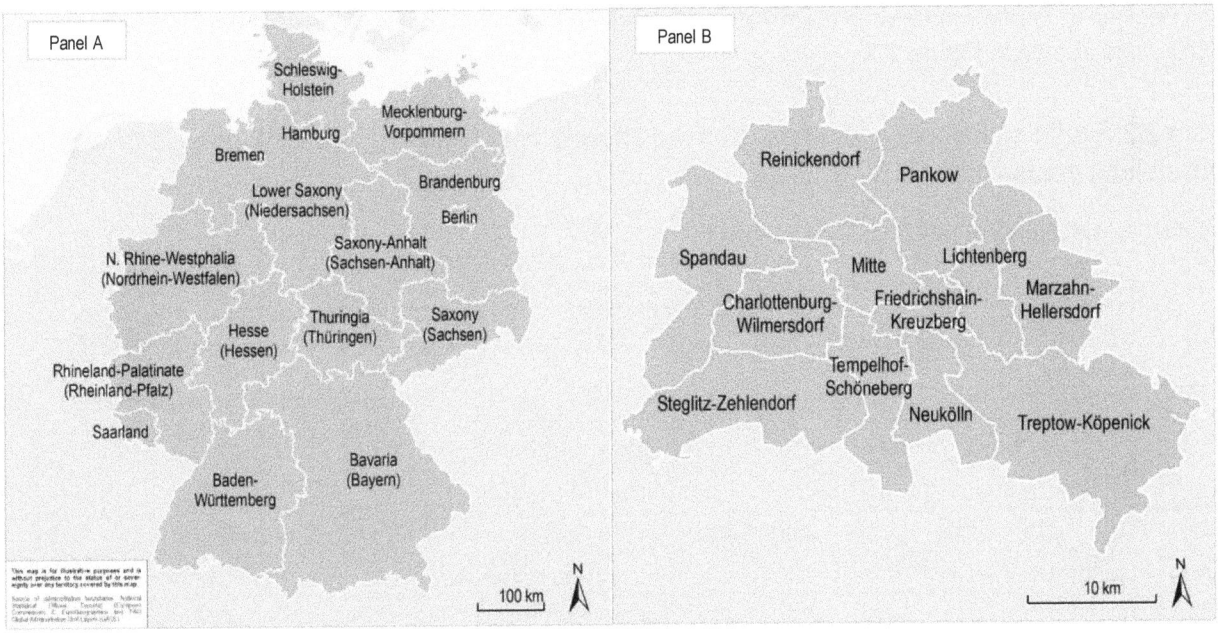

Source: OECD illustration based on administrative boundaries provided by national statistics offices and Eurostat. Copyright of the underlying shapefiles: EuroGeographics and FAO Global Administrative Unit Layers (GAUL).

Like other German federal states, Berlin has legislative power in some domains, such as education, but does not have fiscal autonomy. The German federal states do not raise their own taxes but only collect these. Public revenues are allocated to the federal states using a formula that takes into account the total population and the regional Gross Domestic Product (GDP). Importantly, the German federal system assigns large responsibility to the federal states in the field of initial education (including, to a large extent, tertiary education). Federal statutes regulate other areas within the field of education, such as Germany's dual education system and the continuing education and training (CET) of adults. CET measures implemented on the federal state level thus complement those by the federal government, a system discussed in more detail in section 3. Politically, Berlin's mayor also serves as the federal state's prime minister. Berlin's Senate acts as the city and regional government and the Senators correspond to state Ministers (OECD, 2010[1]). The different *Senatsverwaltungen* ("Senate Departments") correspond to state Ministries.

Berlin's economy and labour market reflect its highly diverse and dynamic population. Berlin, as Germany's largest city was host to nationals from 193 countries in 2020. Its historic division into an East and a West German part further adds to its diversity even among German nationals. The high population growth – between 2000 and 2019, Berlin's population grew by almost 8% – is partly explained by its attractiveness to internal migrants from across Germany. Berlin's labour market reflects some of its dynamism, posing distinct opportunities and challenges to the provision of adult learning. The remainder of this section provides a high-level overview of recent trends in Berlin's labour market and describes the socio-economic profile of its population in more detail.

Berlin has experienced a recent boom in the labour market

Berlin's unemployment rate has been on a steady decline over the past decade. Before the start of the COVID-19 pandemic, Berlin's unemployment rate declined from 13.0% in 2010 to 5.5% in 2019 (Figure 2.2). Compared to other cities across the OECD, Berlin's unemployment rate was relatively low in 2019, on a par with Stockholm (6.3%) and London (4.6%) and only slightly above the second and third biggest cities of Germany, Hamburg (3.7%) and Munich (2.6%). In absolute terms, the 7.5 percentage point decline in Berlin's unemployment rate between 2010 and 2019 was the highest drop among the OECD cities shown in Figure 2.2.

Figure 2.2. Berlin's unemployment rate dropped sharply between 2010 and 2019 relative to major metropolitan areas in the OECD

Percentage of labour force (aged 15 to 64 years)

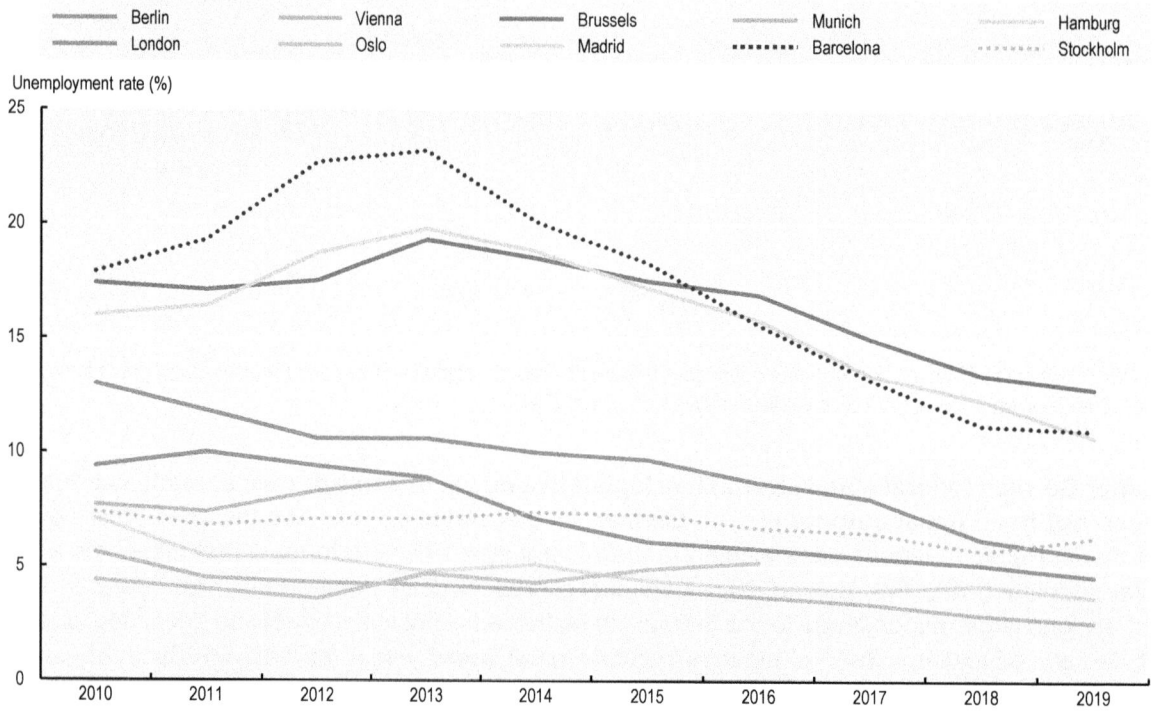

Note: The data correspond to the TL2 regions that compose the respective metropolitan area.
Source: OECD Regional Database.

However, Berlin's unemployment rate remains the highest in Germany when compared to the other German federal states. Figure 2.3 shows Berlin's unemployment rate in national comparison over the period from 2010 to 2020. Unemployment rates dropped across all German federal states over the past decade. The federal states that started at the highest level of unemployment in 2010 – Berlin, Mecklenburg-

Vorpommern, Sachsen and Sachsen-Anhalt – experienced the sharpest drops in their unemployment rate, leading to convergence across German regions. However, despite Berlin's significant labour market improvements, Berlin's unemployment rate remains the highest in Germany. In 2020, the first year of the COVID-19 pandemic, the unemployment rate in Berlin was 6.4%, 1 percentage point higher than in 2019. All other German federal states (excluding Bremen) recorded unemployment rates below 5% in 2020 and only Hamburg (+1.2 percentage points), Brandenburg (+1.1 percentage points) and Rheinland-Pfalz (+1 percentage point) experienced an equally large or larger year-on-year increase in unemployment during the first year of the COVID-19 pandemic.

Figure 2.3. Berlin's unemployment rate remains the highest among Germany's federal states

Percentage of labour force (aged 15 to 64 years)

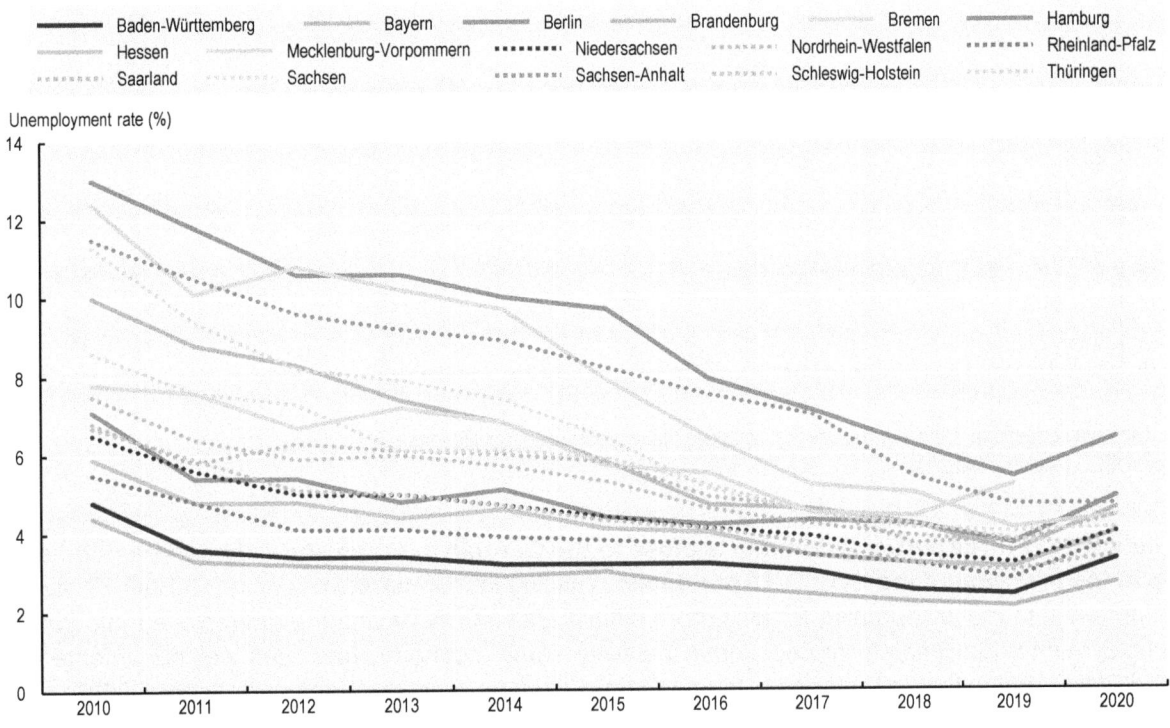

Note: 2020 data for Bremen not available.
Source: OECD Regional Database.

Berlin's labour force participation rate increased significantly before the COVID-19 pandemic, both in absolute terms and in comparison to other European cities. The second important headline figure on regional labour markets is the labour force participation rate. It is defined as the share of the working-age population that is employed or unemployed and seeking for work, and thus captures the share of working-age people who are economically active. Figure 2.4 shows that Berlin's labour force participation rate increased from 76.0% in 2010 to 79.2% in 2019 and its economic activity is now on a par with other OECD capital cities such as London (78.1% in 2019) and Madrid (76.8% in 2019). Nationally, Berlin's labour force participation almost closed the economic activity gap to both Hamburg (79.5% in 2019) and Munich (80.8% in 2019). The 3.2 percentage point increase in Berlin's labour force participation rate is one of the largest among all OECD cities shown in Figure 2.4. The simultaneous decline in Berlin's unemployment rate over the same period (Figure 2.2) implies that the rise in economic activity was indeed driven by an increase in employment within this age group.

Figure 2.4. Berlin's labour force participation rate is now on a par with other European metropolitan areas

Percentage of population aged 15 to 64 years

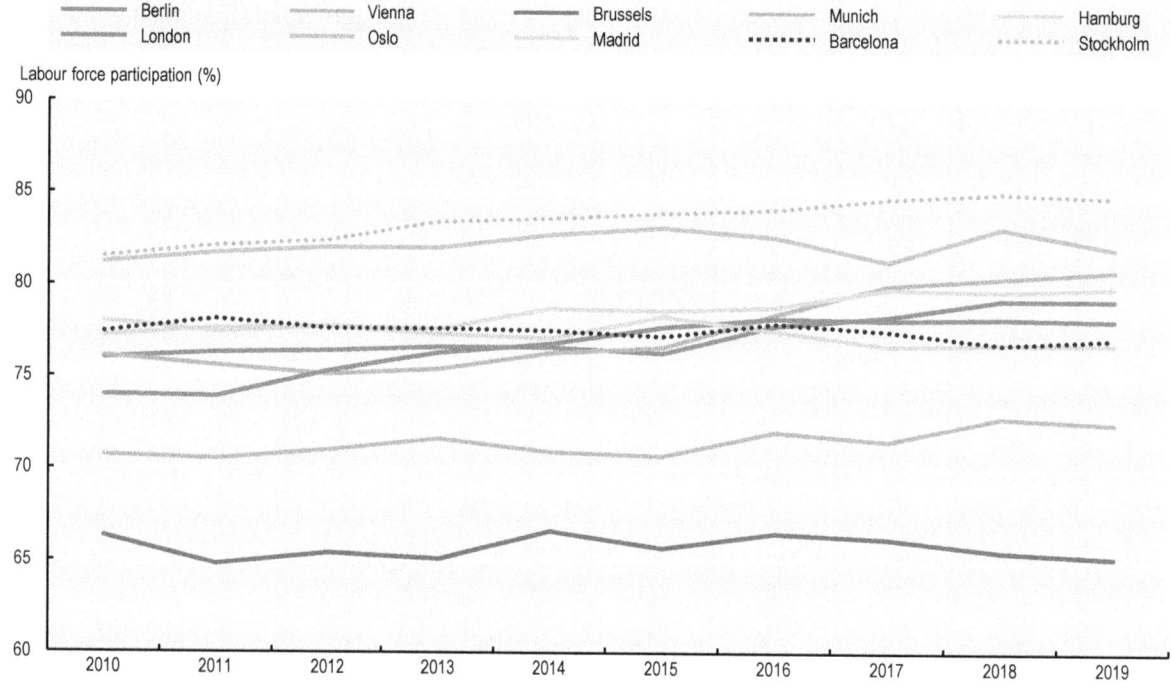

Note: The data correspond to the TL2 regions that compose the respective metropolitan area.
Source: OECD Regional Database.

Berlin's labour force participation rate is close to the German average and only experienced a small drop in the first year of the COVID-19 pandemic. The key labour market risk of the COVID-19 pandemic is its potential to make searching for jobs more difficult, potentially driving the unemployed into long-term unemployment and ultimately into economic inactivity. Such a dynamic has been well documented in the United States during the early stages of the pandemic (Coibion, Gorodnichenko and Weber, 2020[2]). Thus, the COVID-19 pandemic risks leaving longer-lasting scars on the labour force. Berlin's labour force participation rate only experienced a small drop of 0.6 percentage points between 2019 and 2020 (Figure 2.5). Exactly half of the German federal states also showed a drop in economic activity, with Bremen experiencing the largest year-on-year decline of 4.2 percentage points. In 2020, the national-level labour force participation rate stood at 79.2%, only 0.6 percentage points above that of Berlin (78.6%). Over the 2010 to 2020 period, Berlin's 2.6 percentage point increase in labour force participation was around the median among Germany's federal states, with Saarland (+4.3 percentage points) and Bayern (+3.9 percentage points) showing the highest growth rates in their regional labour forces.

Berlin has indeed enjoyed a two decades long boom in employment, in particular in service sectors with many high skill jobs. Between 2000 and 2019, total employment in Berlin grew by an annual rate of almost 1.3%, compared to 0.7% in Germany and 0.6% in the European Union (Figure 2.6). This is equivalent to the creation of almost 450 000 new jobs in Berlin since 2000. The three sectors that recorded the fastest employment growth in Berlin were trade, transport, accommodation and food services (annual growth of 2.4%), financial, insurance, real estate and business activities (annual growth of 1.6%), and public administration, education, health, and arts (annual growth of 1.4%). Those three sectors alone recorded more than 500 000 new jobs. In contrast, employment in industrial jobs or construction fell by 37 000 and 22 000, respectively, making them the sectors with the biggest absolute job losses.

Figure 2.5. Berlin's labour force participation rate is now close to the German average

Percentage of population aged 15 to 64 years

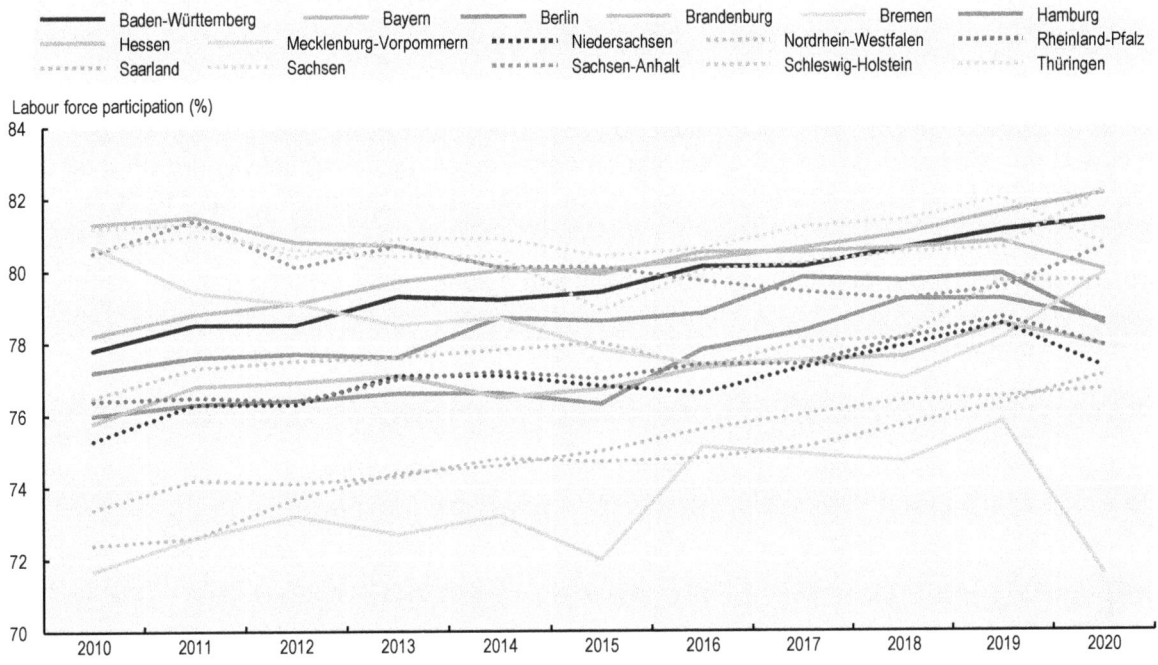

Source: OECD Regional Database.

Figure 2.6. New jobs in Berlin were created mostly in different service sectors

Annual average growth rate in % (Panel A) and absolute change in employment between 2010 and 2019 (Panel B)

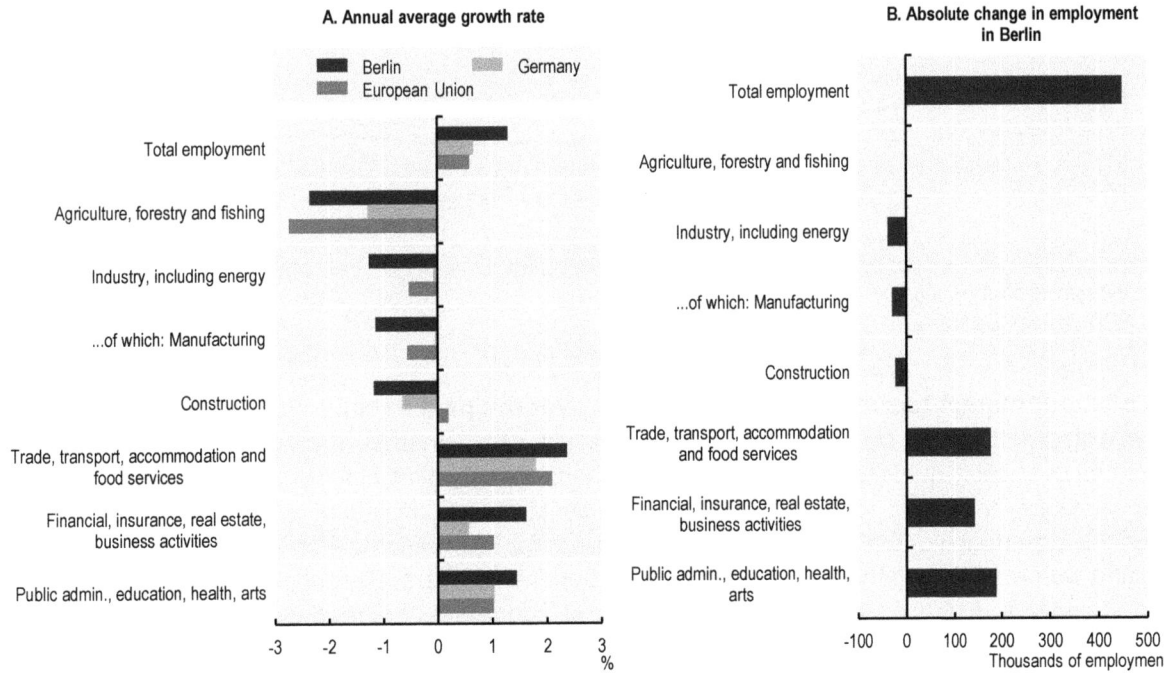

Source: OECD calculations based on OECD Regional database.

Berlin's workforce has become only slightly more productive over the past decade as labour force productivity grew significantly less than in some OECD regions. Stagnation in labour productivity can pose a risk for Berlin's competitiveness as a place of business. Figure 2.7 shows relative changes in regional gross value added per worker against the 2008 base year. In international comparison, Berlin's productivity growth until 2018 was sluggish and only stood at 106% of its productivity per worker in 2008. In other OECD cities such as Oslo (133%), Copenhagen (115%), Barcelona (113%) or Amsterdam (112%), productivity per worker grew significantly more over the same period. As a result, gross value added per worker in Berlin stood at USD 81 107 (constant prices, constant PPP, base year 2015) in 2019, a value much lower than in other major OECD cities that also showed sluggish productivity growth over the past decade, such as Vienna (USD 99 038), Hamburg (USD 104 051) or Stockholm (USD 110 507).

Figure 2.7. Berlin's labour productivity rose slowly since 2008

Changes in regional gross value added per worker against 2008 base year

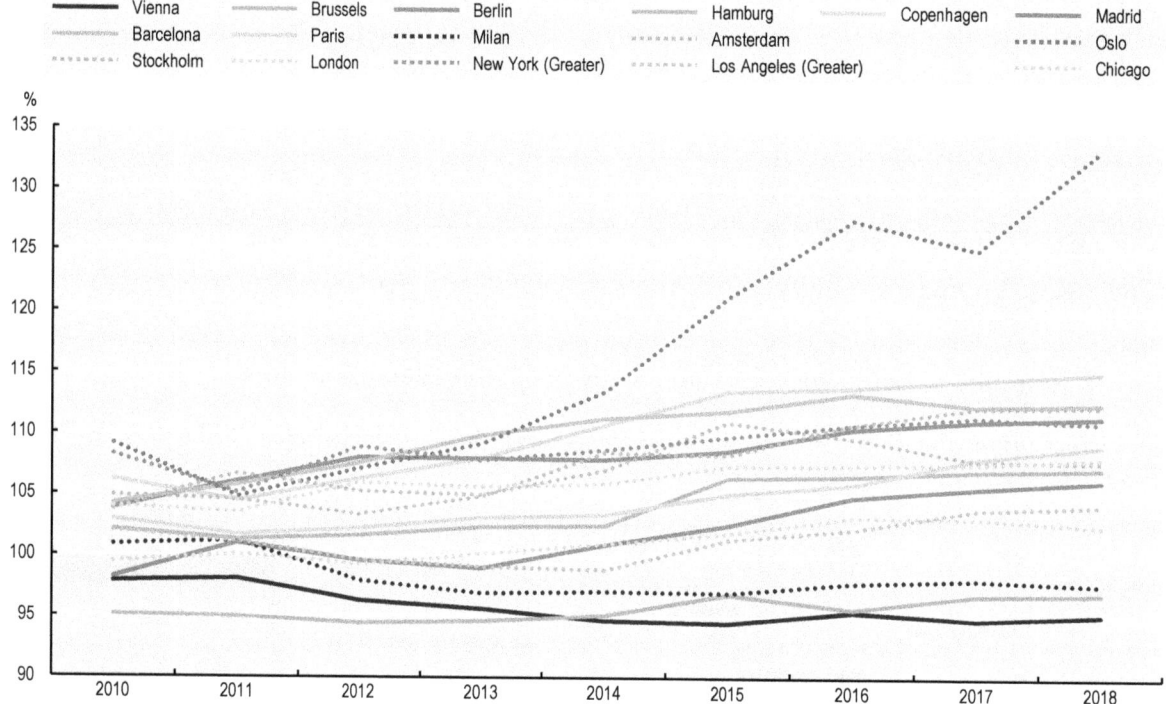

Note: Labour productivity is measured by GDP per worker in USD, constant prices, constant PPP, base year 2015. All values are presented relative to the starting point in 2008.
Source: OECD Regional Database.

Berlin's labour market has significantly tightened over the past decade. Following a decade of rapid employment growth driven by the service sector, Berlin's labour market has now entered a new period. Recruitment of suitably qualified workers will become increasingly difficult for employers, ultimately putting upward pressure on wages in sectors that experience shortages in labour supply. Such development elevates the importance of the local adult learning system for two reasons: First, it can increase the supply of qualified workers that can meet the skills needs of Berlin employers. Second, as wages are likely to rise disproportionally in high-skill sectors, there is a risk of aggravated social divisions if low and medium-educated workers are not trained and upskilled to remain attractive to local employers.

Labour demand indicators indeed suggest that Berlin's labour market will soon face a period of greater difficulties in recruitment and upward pressure on wages in sectors that experience labour shortages. Figure 2.8 and Figure 2.9 show the number of job vacancies and the number of unemployed per job vacancy in Berlin and Brandenburg in comparison to the other German federal states. Figure 2.8 shows that the total number of job vacancies in Berlin has increased between 2010 and 2020, rising from 39 800 in 2010 to 113 600 in 2019, followed by a drop to 92 400 during 2020, the first year of the COVID-19 pandemic. Most other German federal states experienced a similar increase in absolute vacancies, with differences mostly explained by different population sizes across regions. However, such absolute rise in labour demand needs to be compared to the supply side of the labour market, best measured by the available workforce. Figure 2.9 shows that, relative the jobseeker-per-vacancy ratio dropped significantly in Berlin. In 2010, approximately nine unemployed workers were available for each open position. By 2019, that ratio had dropped to slightly above one unemployed worker per vacancy and then rose to approximately two unemployed workers per job vacancy in 2020, the first year of the COVID-19 pandemic. The other German federal states experienced a similar tightening of their labour market, albeit at a less rapid pace than Berlin.

Figure 2.8. The total number of vacancies in Berlin increased between 2010 and 2019

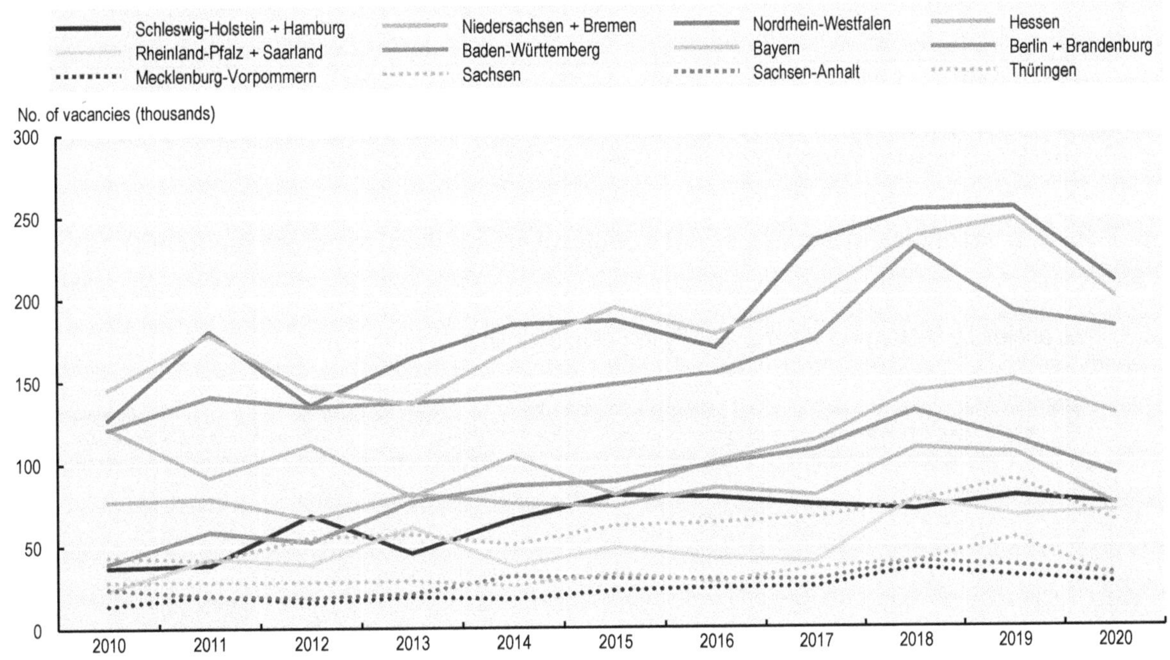

Note: 2020 data is preliminary.
Source: IAB – Institute for Employment Research, Job Vacancy Survey.

Berlin's service sector drove the increase in labour demand. The employment growth in the service sector is also reflected by a sectoral decomposition of a direct labour demand measure, the number of job vacancies. Figure 2.10 shows the total number of job vacancies disaggregated by the sector of economic activity in Berlin between 2010 and 2020. The service sector, both business and other services, experienced by far the largest rise in absolute job openings. Vacancies in the business service sector rose from 12 000 in 2010 to 26 000 in 2019. Similarly, job vacancies in other services – which includes services related to human health and social services, education services, arts, entertainment and recreation as well as accommodation and food services – increased from 13 000 in 2010 to 43 000 in 2019. The construction sector (+11 100 vacancies between 2010 and 2019) and the information and communication sectors (+4 400) also experienced a rise in labour demand.

Figure 2.9. Berlin's labour market tightened significantly between 2010 and 2019

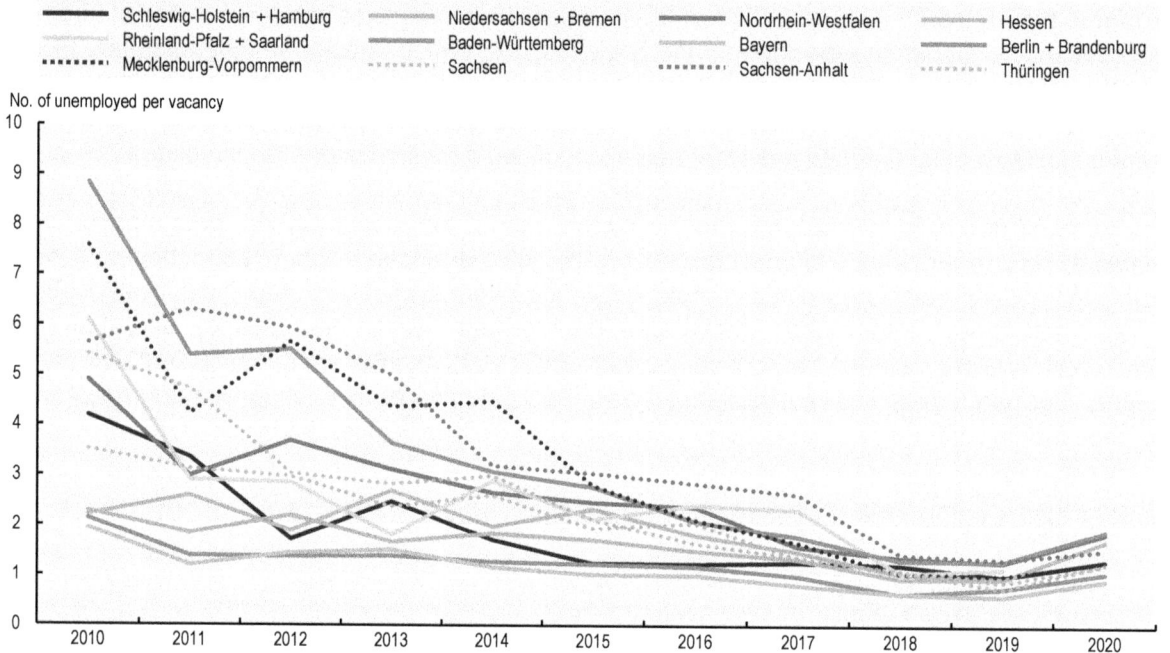

Note: Unemployed refers to all unemployed aged 15 to 64 and is an estimation based on EU-LFS data. 2020 data is preliminary.
Source: IAB – Institute for Employment Research, Job Vacancy Survey and OECD Regional Database.

Figure 2.10. Job vacancies in Berlin's service sector were on the rise before the COVID-19 pandemic

Number of vacancies by sector of economic activity in Berlin over time

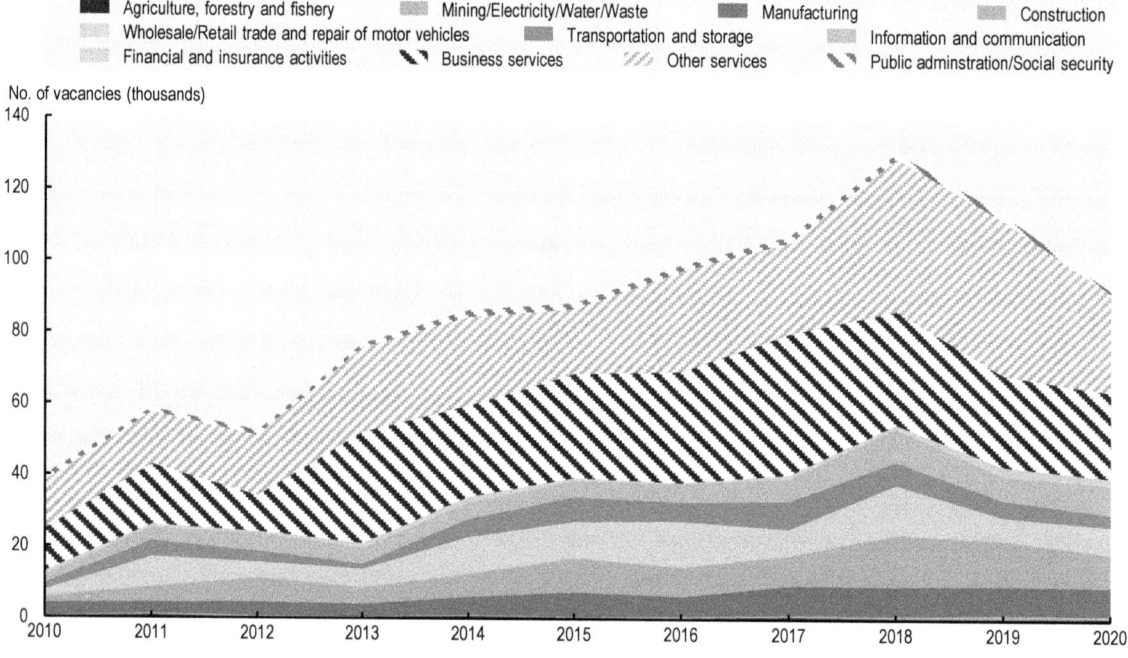

Note: Economic activities classified following ISIC Rev. 4. 2020 data is preliminary.
Source: IAB – Institute for Employment Research, Job Vacancy Survey.

Already before the COVID-19 pandemic, a growing number of businesses in Berlin struggled to fill vacancies. The share of Berlin's and Brandenburg's companies that reported difficulties in finding a suitable candidate during the hiring procedure increased from 30.0% in 2010 to 40.6% in 2019 (Figure 2.11). The increased difficulties in hiring reported by companies follows the trend in Germany as a whole: Over the same period, the share of German companies reporting difficulties during the hiring procedure rose from 29.1% to 44.0%. The drop in the share of vacancies companies had difficulties to fill observed between 2019 and 2020 across all German federal states but Schleswig-Holstein and Hamburg can likely be ascribed to the selective decrease in hiring for positions that are relatively harder to fill.

Figure 2.11. The share of companies struggling to fill vacancies increased across Germany over the past decade

Share of vacancies companies had difficulties filling, by German federal states, 2010-2020

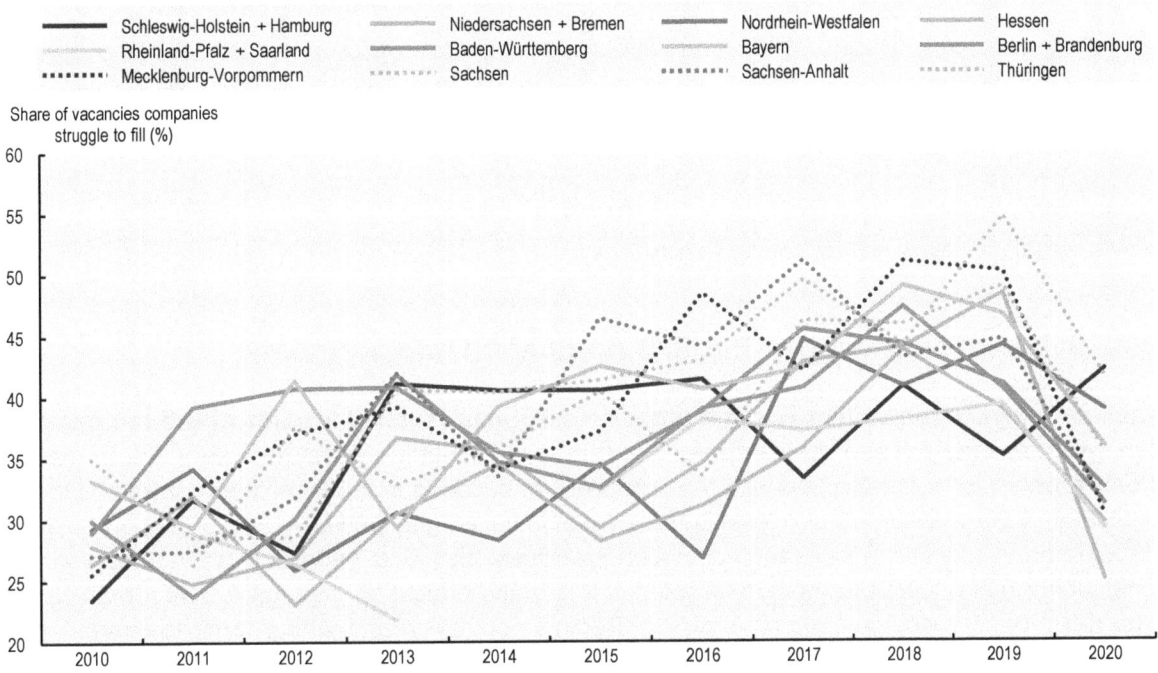

Note: Companies are first asked to consider the last time when a new employee was hired (within the past 12 months). They are then asked if they experienced difficulties in finding a suitable candidate during the hiring procedure. 2020 data is preliminary.
Source: IAB – Institute for Employment Research, Job Vacancy Survey.

An insufficient number of applicants and an insufficient professional qualification of candidates are increasingly the main reasons why companies struggle to fill job vacancies. Figure 2.12 shows the self-assessed reasons companies mention when asked about why they experience difficulties to find suitable candidates for job openings. In 2010, Berlin's companies stated that they struggled filling 17.7% of job vacancies due to insufficient professional qualification of the candidate. In 2019, the share of vacancies they struggled to fill for the same reason rose to 26.4%. Similarly, the share of vacancies Berlin's companies struggled to fill due to an insufficient number of applications rose from 17.1% in 2010 to 26.1% in 2019. Other reasons, such as the unwillingness of applicants to accept the workload (+5.7 percentage points between 2010 and 2019) and excessive salary demands (+9.0 percentage) points also increased significantly but were mentioned less frequently. The drop in the share of vacancies companies struggled to fill between 2019 and 2020 can once again likely be ascribed to selective hiring during the COVID-19 pandemic.

Figure 2.12. Berlin's companies increasingly struggle to find suitable candidates

Share of vacancies companies in Berlin had difficulties filling, by reason, 2010-2020

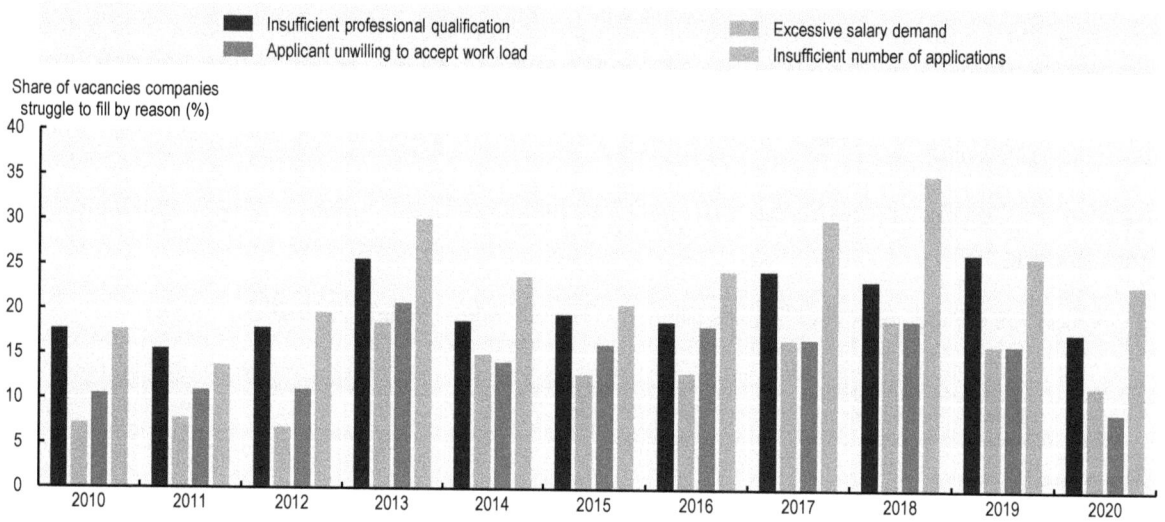

Note: Multiple (or no) answer(s) possible so percentages do not add up to 100%. 2020 data is preliminary. The denominator is the total number of vacancies.
Source: IAB – Institute for Employment Research, Job Vacancy Survey.

Social divisions characterise Berlin's population and economy

The above analysis shows that Berlin's labour market has reached a point where the demand for skilled workers may exceed their supply. For this reason, Berlin's policy makers have to make sure their entire labour force is equipped with the right skills to succeed in the local labour market. One of the key indicators for a workforce's skill level is the level of initial education. However, to support upskilling in the labour force, identifying relevant population characteristics and geographical variation within the regional labour market can also help in targeting training and education measures. The remainder of this chapter describes the socio-economic profile of Berlin's population and labour force to characterise the regional labour supply side, with a particular focus on Berlin's young adults and its diverse migrant population.

The average level of education in Berlin is higher than in other German regions, but lower than in major cities across the OECD. Figure 2.13 shows that among Berlin's 25 to 64 year old population, 13% fell into the low education category in 2020, defined as individuals whose formal education is below upper secondary education. Forty-three percent had attained a medium level of education, defined as an attainment of upper secondary but non-tertiary education. Forty-two percent of Berlin's population had attained tertiary education and are therefore considered highly educated. Panel A of Figure 2.13 shows that Berlin's share of highly-educated individuals is the highest among Germany's federal states. On the other hand, the share of low-educated individuals falls right on the median among Germany's regions. However, academic research has long established that highly educated individuals are drawn to cities in relatively larger number for better income opportunities (see Brinkman (2015[3]) for a summary). Thus, it is insightful to compare the level of education in Berlin's population to large cities across the OECD. Panel B shows that Berlin's share of highly educated is relatively low when compared to other OECD cities. Vienna (42.7%), Brussels (49.3%), Madrid (50.2%), Stockholm (53.7%), Oslo (54.9%) and London (68.4%) all have a larger share of highly educated than Berlin among its 25 to 64 year olds. Berlin, on the other hand, has the largest share of individuals educated at a medium level (43%) compared to the cities displayed.

Figure 2.13. Education profile of Berlin's working-age population in national and international comparison

Population aged 25 to 64 in 2020

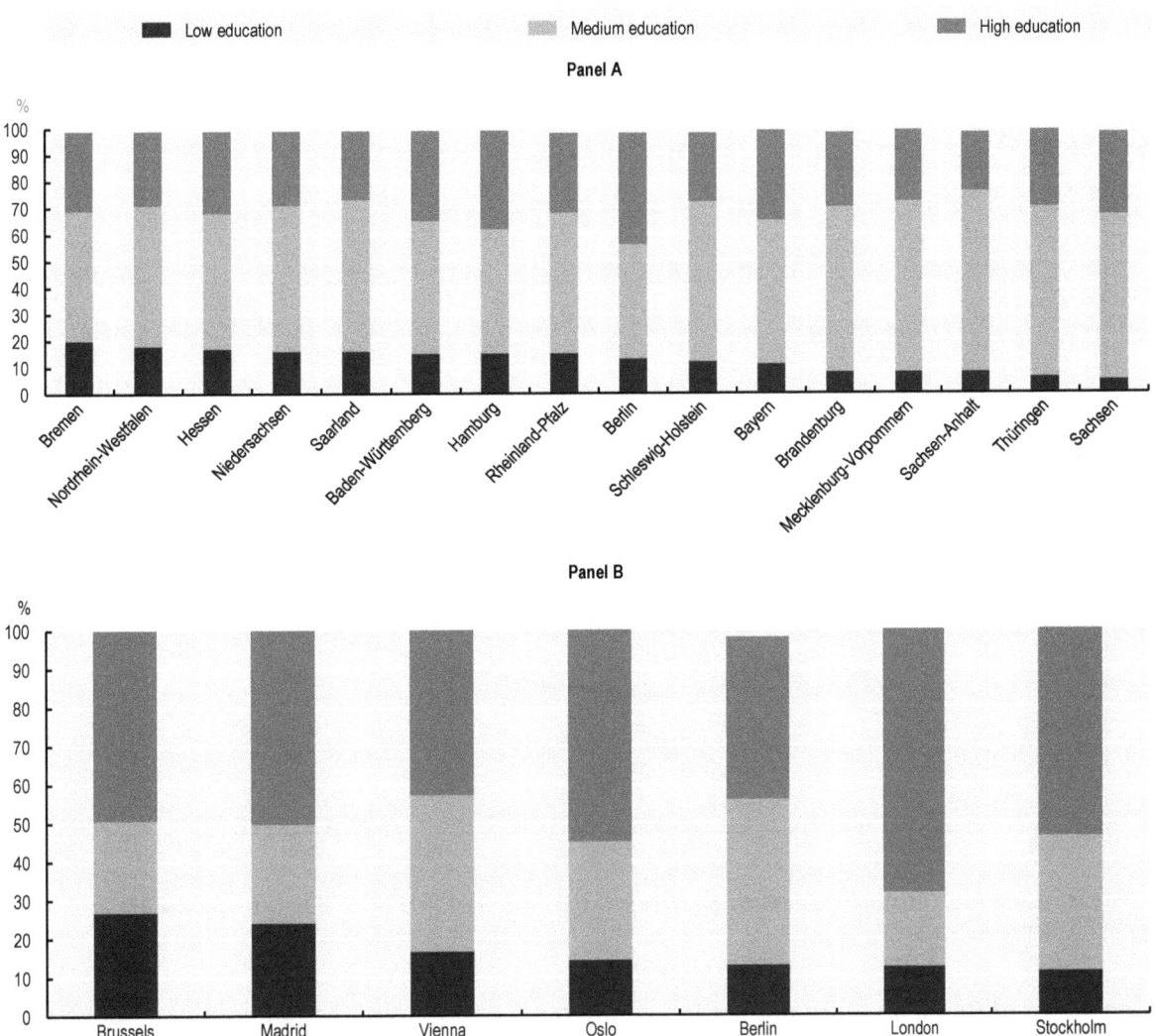

Note: Low education corresponds to a level of education below upper secondary education (ISCED2011 level 0-2). A medium level of education corresponds to upper secondary but non-tertiary education (ISCED2011 level 3-4). A high level of education corresponds to tertiary education (ISCED2011 level 5-8).
Source: OECD Regional Database.

The share of early leavers from education and training is high in Berlin compared to other German regions. The level of education among young adults can be a good indicator for the future of regional labour supply. Figure 2.14 shows the share of individuals aged 18 to 24 who finished no more than lower secondary education and are not involved in further education or training in Berlin, compared to other German regions. In 2018, this number stood at 13.6% in Berlin, second only to Bremen, where an even larger share of young adults fell into the low education category (14.6%). The German average stood at 10.3% in the same year. Over the 2010 to 2018 period, Berlin saw little improvement in its rate of early leavers from education and training. The share of early leavers from education and training only decreased by 0.8 percentage points over the observed period compared to a 1.5 percentage point decline in Germany as a whole.

Figure 2.14. Berlin has one of the highest rates of early leavers from education and training in Germany

Share of individuals aged 18 to 24 who finished no more than lower secondary education and are not involved in further education or training

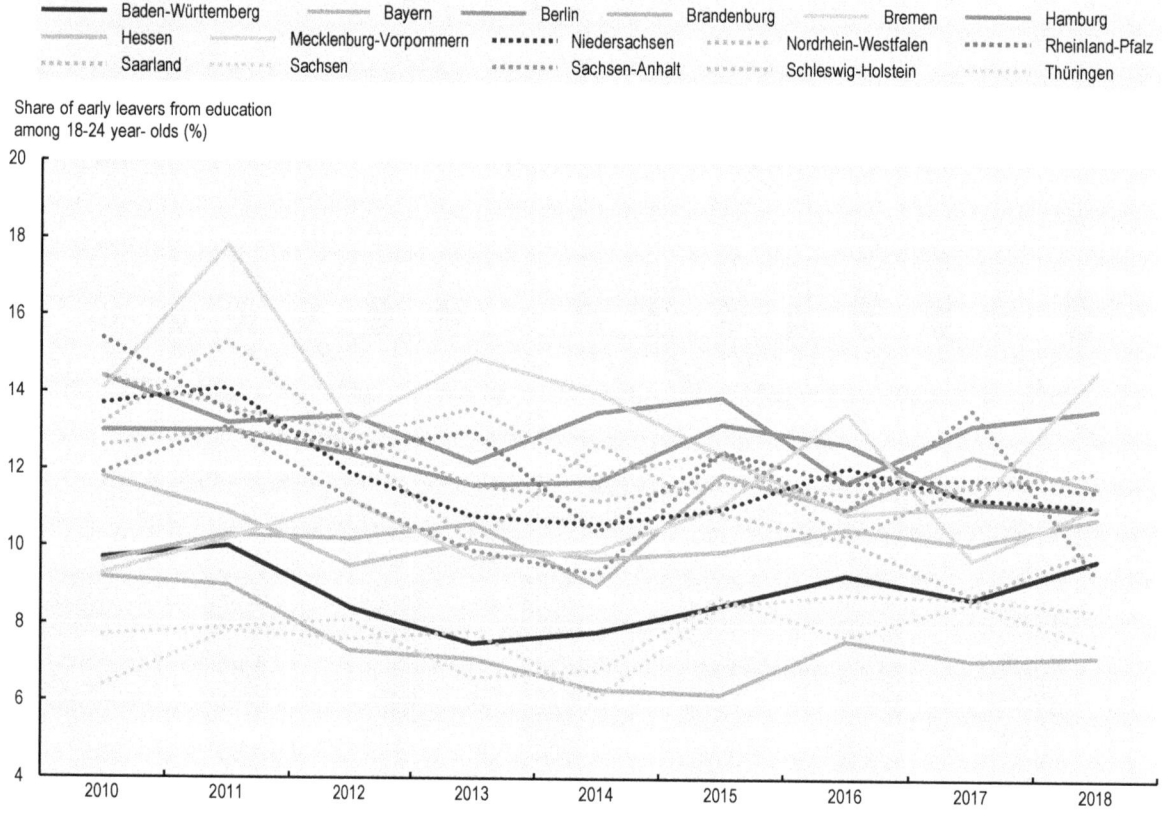

Note: The early leavers rate is expressed as a percentage of the total population aged 18 to 24. 2018 is latest data available.
Source: OECD Regional Database.

A large share of Berlin's young population is not in education and unemployed or inactive (NEET). A complementary indicator to the share of early leavers from education and training is the NEET rate, which is defined as the share of 18 to 24 year olds who are not currently in education and unemployed or inactive (NEET). For example, OECD research has shown that differences in literacy skill growth across the OECD are strongly related to the NEET rate. Conversely, reductions in NEET rates result in decreased disparities in achievement on literacy tests and decrease intergenerational transmission of educational advantages (OECD, 2021[4]). In 2019, the NEET rate among Berlin's young adults stood at 10.2%, well above the German average of 7.7% and third only to the two other city states of Hamburg (11.0%) and Bremen (12.0%) among Germany's federal states. Despite the relatively high NEET rate in Berlin, the trend between 2010 and 2019 shows a relatively large drop of 5.1 percentage points, the third highest improvement across German federal states. Thus, recent cohorts of 18 to 24 year olds are more likely to be in education or employment than previous cohorts.

Figure 2.15. A large share of Berlin's young population is not in education and unemployed or inactive (NEET)

Share of 18-24 year-old population not in education and unemployed or inactive (NEET)

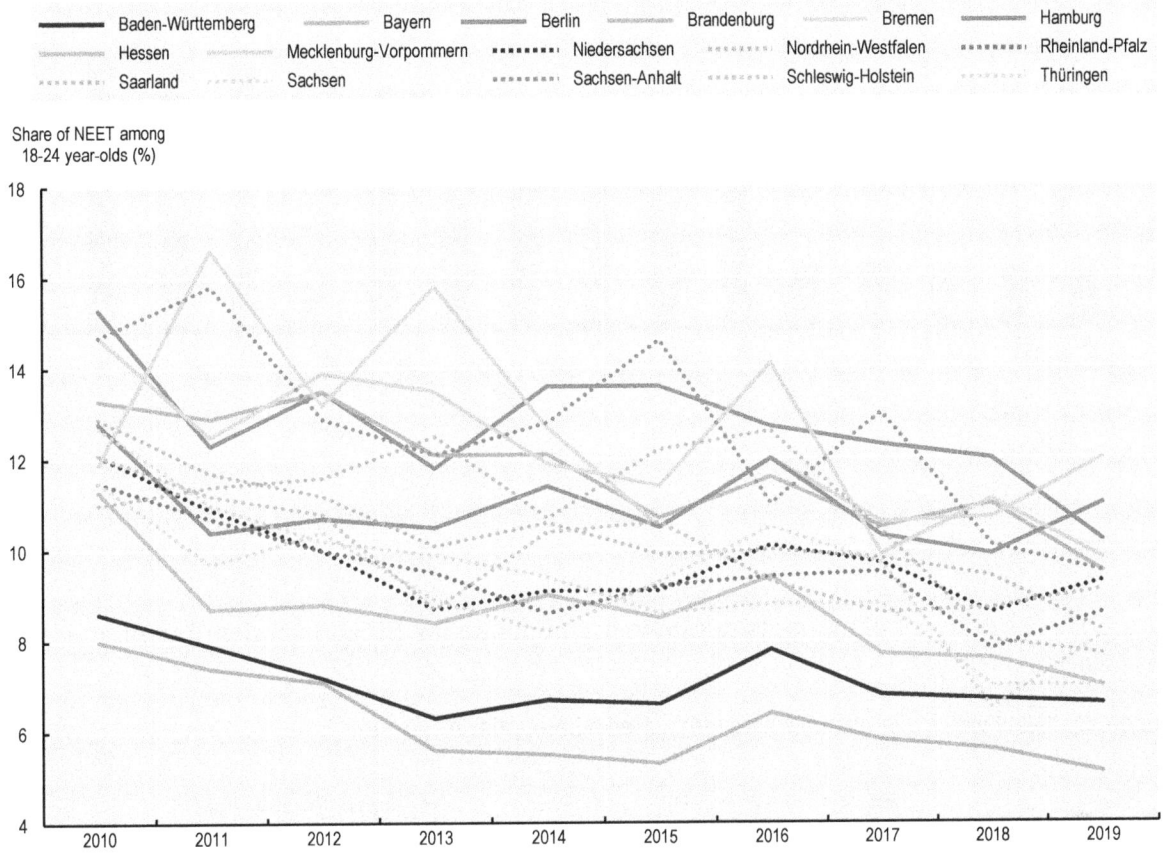

Source: OECD Regional Database.

A distinct feature of Berlin's population is its diversity. In 2020, Berlin was host to nationals from 193 countries. Figure 2.16 shows that the share of Berlin's population with a migration background stood at 33.1% in 2019. Only the federal states of Bremen (36.5%), Hessen (34.4%), Hamburg (33.9%) and Baden-Württemberg (33.8%) had marginally higher populations with migration background in relative terms. In all other German regions, a significantly lower share of the regional populations had a migration background in 2019. For the purposes of this report, migration background is defined as either not having German citizenship, or at least one parent not holding German citizenship by birth.

Migrants are spread highly unevenly across Berlin's boroughs. Similar to the settlement patterns in the whole of Germany, Berlin's migrants are mostly settled in Berlin's former Western parts for historical reasons (Figure 2.17). In Berlin-Mitte, which was divided into an Eastern and a Western part before the German reunification, 54% of the population had a migration background in 2021, compared to 18% in Treptow-Köpenick. Other boroughs with large migrant populations are Neukölln and Friedrichshain-Kreuzberg. Individuals with a migration background from outside the EU constitute the largest share of the total population with a migration background in all of Berlin's boroughs.

Figure 2.16. Migrants in Germany predominantly live in West German cities

Share of population with a migration background by German federal states in 2019

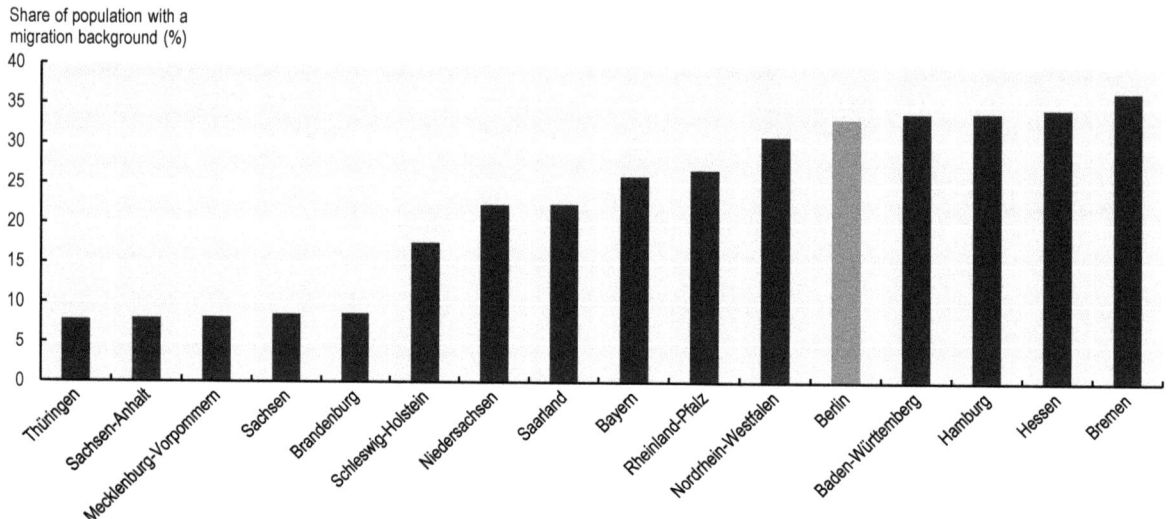

Note: Migration background defined as either (i) no German citizenship or (ii) at least one parent does not hold German citizenship by birth.
Source: Federal Institute for Population Research.

Figure 2.17. The majority of migrants originate from outside the EU and are distributed unevenly across Berlin

Share of population with a migration background by Berlin boroughs, 2021

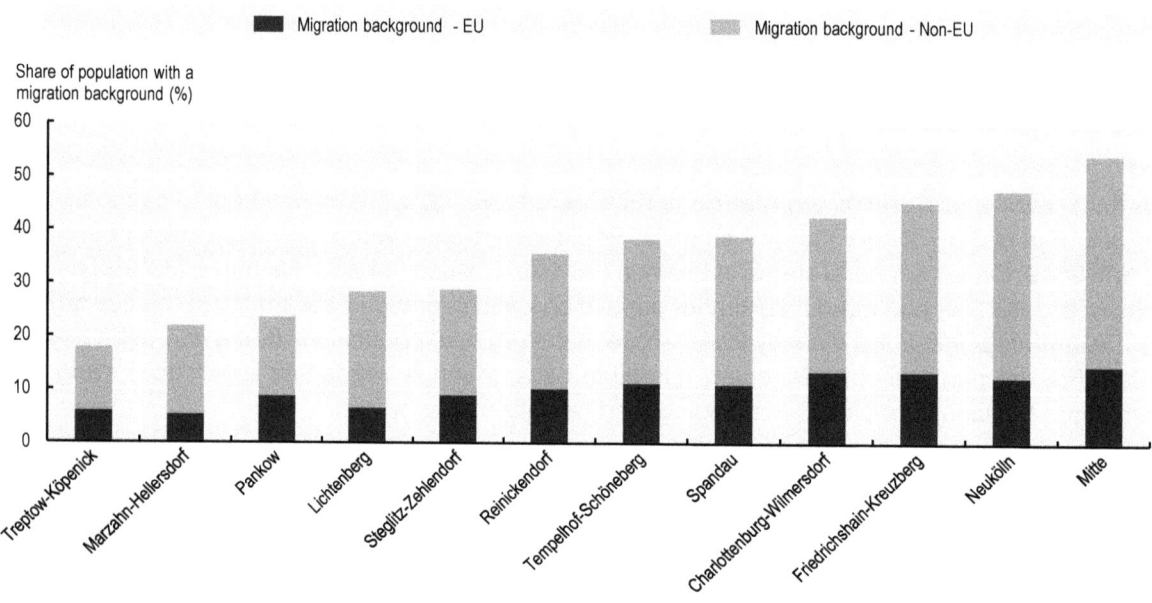

Note: Migration background defined as either (i) no German citizenship or (ii) at least one parent does not hold German citizenship by birth.
Source: Statistics office Berlin-Brandenburg based on population register (*Einwohnerregisterstatistik*).

The labour market attachment of Berlin's population with a migration background is lower in all boroughs. Figure 2.18 shows the labour force participation and the unemployment rate in Berlin's boroughs among the population aged 15 to 64 by migration background in 2019. Panel A shows that the labour force participation of Berlin's population with a migration background is lower in all of its boroughs. On average, 72% of those with a migration background were economically active, compared to 83% among Germans without a migration background. Similarly, Panel B shows that the unemployment rate among Germans without a migration background stood at 4% in Berlin, compared to 9% among those with a migration background. Taken together, Figure 2.18 shows that Berlin's population with a migration background has a significantly lower labour market attachment. The uneven spatial distribution of Berlin's population with a migration background across the city therefore provides a partial explanation for differences in headline labour market indicators.

Figure 2.18. The labour market attachment of migrants is relatively low in all of Berlin's boroughs

Population aged 15 to 64, 2019

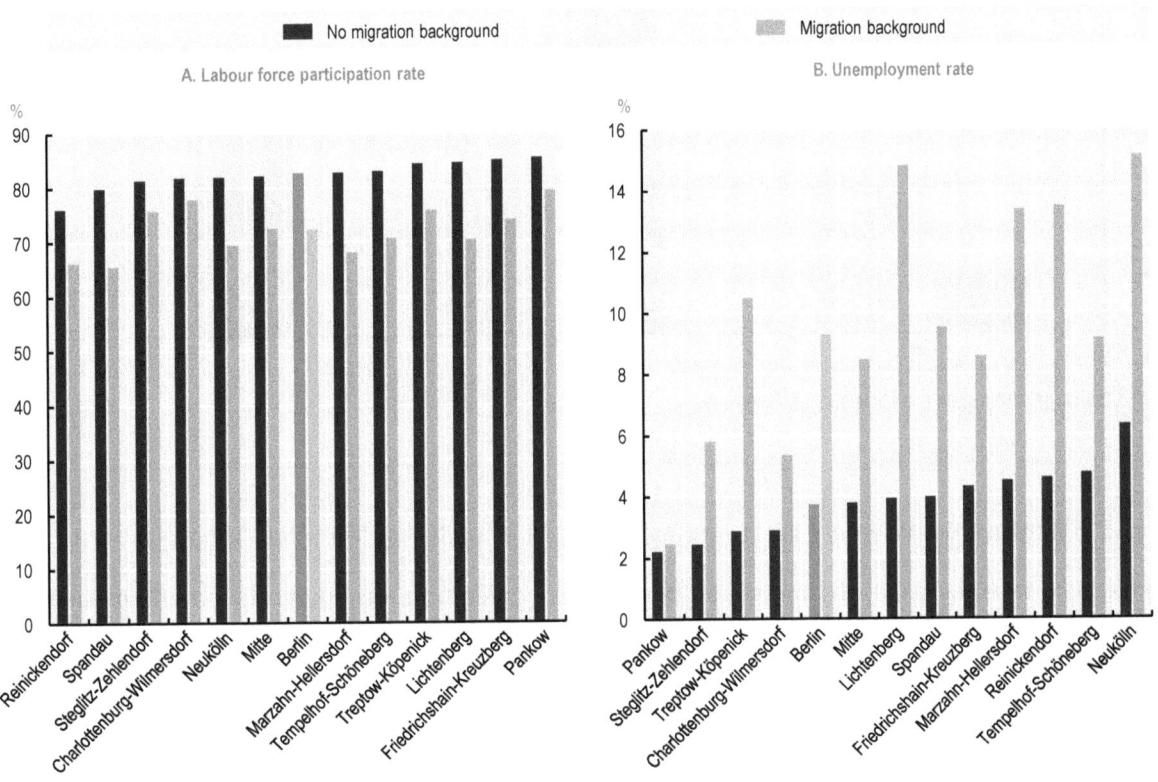

Note: Migration background defined as either (i) no German citizenship or (ii) at least one parent does not hold German citizenship by birth.
Source: OECD elaboration on the Microcensus Germany.

One reason for the relatively low labour force participation and the relatively high unemployment rate among people with a migration background is the lower average level of education in that segment of the population. Figure 2.19 shows the educational attainment in Berlin's population by migration background. In 2019, 24.8% of Berlin's population aged 25 or older with a migration background fell into the low education category, compared to 8.3% among those without a migration background. The share of the population with a migration background holding a medium level of formal education stood at 33.2%, compared to 51.2% among Germans without a migration background. 42.0% of those with a migration background had attained a high level of education, which is higher than the rate of the German population, which stands at 40.5%. The higher incidence of low education among Berlin's population with a migration background constitutes a likely reason for the lower labour market attachment of this group. However, as explained in more detail in Box 2.1, migrants also face distinct challenges on the labour market. The non-transferability of degrees across borders, lacking local language skills and lacking citizenship can all have a negative effect on employment prospects also for those with high educational attainment.

Figure 2.19. A relatively large share of Berlin's migrants fall into the low education category

Educational attainment by migration background, population aged 25 and above, 2019

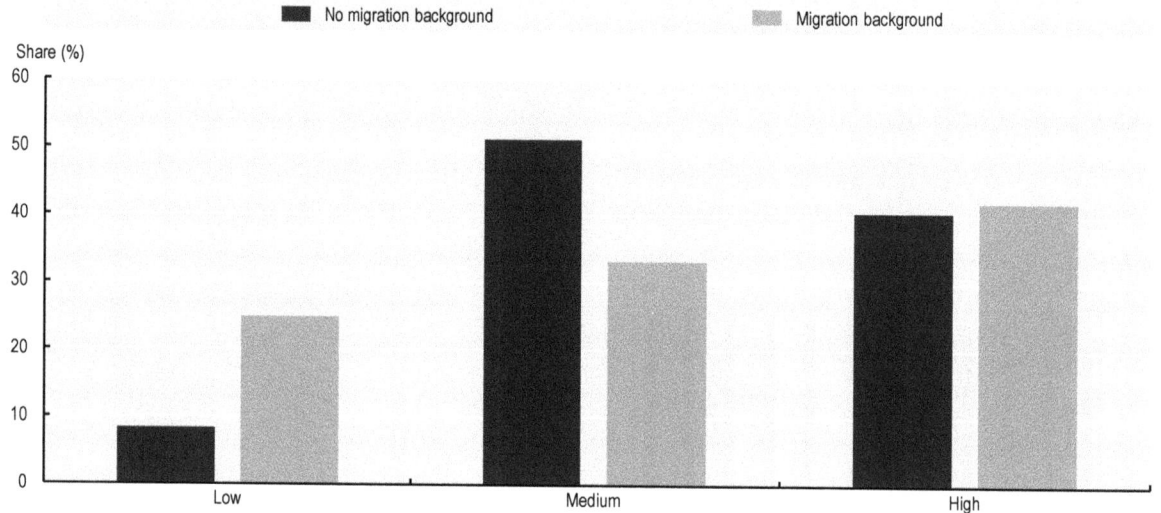

Source: OECD elaboration on the Microcensus Germany.

Box 2.1. Why are employment rates among migrants often lower than that of native-born?

Three main reasons exist why migrants often show a lower labour market attachment, measured by labour force participation and employment rates. For each of these reasons, policy measures exist that can help the integration of migrants into the labour market.

The first reason is the non-transferability of degrees across borders due to differences in quality and content of education. Foreign education and even the training for specific occupations may differ from country to country, partly due to country-specific job requirements and partly due to the differences in the quality of those teaching job-related skills. A closely intertwined issue is the signalling value of foreign degrees: Employers are typically less familiar with education attained abroad and may therefore put a discount on foreign degrees when making hiring decisions. Policy efforts to acknowledge foreign degrees formally and offer retraining measures if degrees are below the national standard for the respective occupation can help migrants' chances on the domestic labour market.

The second reason is the lack of language skills. A range of academic studies have shown that knowledge of the destination country's official language is causally linked to higher labour force participation, employment and wages among immigrants. Offering language courses that allow migrants to take up jobs that require interactions in the destination country's official language can therefore greatly benefit their labour market attachment.

The third reason is the lack of citizenship. Not holding the nationality of the country a person resides in may have negative effects on their labour market attachment through a number of channels. Employment options in the public sector may be limited to citizens of the country, the weaker signalling values of foreign nationality may affect hiring decisions, discrimination among employers and – among some groups of migrants – certainty regarding the duration of stay may all play a role. Easing naturalization processes may therefore benefit the employment of migrants.

Source: Summary based on Ludolph (2021[5]), *The Value of Formal Host-Country Education for the Labour Market Position of Refugees: Evidence from Austria.*

References

Brinkman, J. (2015), "Big Cities and the Highly Educated: What's the Connection?", *Federal Reserve Bank of Philadelphia Research Department*. [3]

Coibion, O., Y. Gorodnichenko and M. Weber (2020), "Labor Markets During the COVID-19 Crisis: A Preliminary View", National Bureau of Economic Research, Cambridge, MA, http://dx.doi.org/10.3386/w27017. [2]

Ludolph, L. (2021), *The Value of Formal Host-Country Education for the Labour Market Position of Refugees: Evidence from Austria*, https://papers.ssrn.com/sol3/papers.cfm?abstract_id=3904543. [5]

OECD (2021), *OECD Skills Outlook 2021: Learning for Life*, OECD Publishing, Paris, https://dx.doi.org/10.1787/0ae365b4-en. [4]

OECD (2010), *Higher Education in Regional and City Development - Berlin, Germany*, https://www.oecd.org/germany/45359278.pdf (accessed on 19 January 2022). [1]

3 The impact of the future of work on Berlin's labour market

This chapter analyses the main trends, challenges and opportunities for the labour market in Berlin. It focuses on four dimensions: i) the effects of automation; ii) the consequences of digitalisation and the transition to a low-carbon economy; iii) the rise of non-standard work; and (iv) the changing demand for skills during the COVID-19 pandemic. In doing so, the chapter benchmarks Berlin with other regions in Germany and with selected comparable metropolitan areas across OECD countries.

In Brief

Automation and digitalisation are changing Berlin's labour market profoundly and are driving the increasingly rapid transformation of the world of work

- **The COVID-19 pandemic has accelerated megatrends such as automation and digitalisation.** A wide body of evidence shows that firms are more likely to invest in automation following economic crisis periods. Amid lockdowns and social distancing measures, firms and employees in Berlin have embraced remote-working and digital tools, thus speeding up the process of digitalisation.
- **Automation could transform Berlin's labour market.** Risks of automation mainly affect workers in low- or medium-skill occupations because automation is a skills-biased technological change that mainly benefits and complements high-skilled workers. Combined with COVID-19, the impacts of automation could be a double whammy on disadvantaged groups, entrenching inequality in Berlin.
- **Automation threatens almost half of all jobs in Berlin.** According to OECD estimates, 14% of jobs in Berlin are highly automatable, with a probability of automation of over 70%. At 32%, the share of jobs that have a significant risk of being strongly affected by automation is even higher. Those jobs are likely to see significant changes in their tasks and the required skill sets for these tasks, necessitating learning and training opportunities for those workers that are most at risk.
- **Many people have in non-standard work arrangements in Berlin, consisting of self-employed, part-time and temporary work.** The rise of non-standard work offers new opportunities for some, such as greater compatibility of family and professional life, or an easier transition into the labour market for youth, but creates new challenges for others. In most cases, individuals in non-standard work arrangements have worse social protection, have less access to training and adult learning opportunities, and are generally more vulnerable to economic shocks such as the current COVID-19 pandemic.
- **COVID-19 and digitalisation have led to a change in the demand for skills in Berlin.** Over the course of the pandemic, Berlin experienced a surge in the relative demand for advanced digital skills, such as programming or data analysis. Additionally, basic digital skills appear to be taken for granted in most new jobs. Despite this growing importance, many Berliners lack digital skills, highlighting the need for support programmes that allow workers to gain experience and competence in dealing with an increasingly digital work environment.

Introduction

Across the OECD, megatrends such as digitalisation, automation and artificial intelligence (AI) are contributing to one of the most profound transformation of local labour markets in decades. As elsewhere, these trends will have a strong and lasting impact on Berlin's labour market. While the effects of these trends are already in motion, the COVID-19 pandemic is accelerating digitalisation and automation. With social distancing rules in place, millions of workers have adopted teleworking. It seems likely that a non-negligible degree of teleworking or hybrid working arrangements might prevail beyond the pandemic. Thus, COVID-19 appears to be a catalyst for long-lasting change in the way firms operate and people work as they embrace technological change to find innovative solutions that allow them to work.

Against this backdrop, the changing future of work will come with greater risks for some people and sectors in Berlin than for others. The pandemic has been exacerbating pre-existing structural issues within Berlin's labour market, such as skills gaps, skills imbalances and a polarisation into well-paying and precarious jobs. Sound adult learning and skills development strategies are an essential policy tool that can help address these issues and can ensure that Berlin is prepared for the future of work, and the new types of jobs and alternative work arrangements such as part-time work that are on the rise.

In managing the economic consequences of the crisis and the subsequent recovery, policy makers in Berlin need to provide new solutions. For a strong and sustainable economic recovery, those solutions need to not only address the direct economic effects of the pandemic but also address structural labour market challenges. In analysing these trends and challenges, this chapter has the following structure. First, it examines the impact of automation on Berlin's local labour market. Second, it describes how job polarisation affects the availability of different types of jobs. Finally, it shows trends in the growth of non-standard work, which creates both opportunities and new challenges for individuals.

How does automation affect Berlin's labour market?

Labour markets in OECD countries have undergone significant structural changes over recent decades. Driven by new technologies, products and consumption patterns, a range of new types of jobs have emerged. On the flipside, employment in some traditional industries has declined. As a result, the type of skills that firms seek and workers need to thrive professionally has changed. Global megatrends such as automation and digitalisation that have accelerated during the COVID-19 pandemic will further drive this structural transformation of the economy, leading to a significantly different future of work. The pandemic being a catalyst for change, as firms and employees have embraced new ways of working and collaborating, ranging from sudden rise in remote working to a significant uptake of digital technology and services. These developments, especially since they are likely to continue at least partly, will have a considerable impact on how people work as well as what type of skills they need to have.

Automation threatens almost half of all jobs in Berlin

Automation will cause one of the most significant transformation of labour markets in OECD countries in decades. On the one hand, the automation of production processes offers new opportunities and enhances productivity, thus raising prosperity and living standards. On the other hand, it poses new and unequal risks to workers because it is a skills-biased technological change. It tends to benefit some workers (mainly high-skill) but potentially replaces or strongly changes the jobs of other workers (mainly low-skill or middle-skill). Automation will result in a replacement of certain tasks and jobs, creating a risk that some workers may not enjoy the benefits that automation can generate but instead might struggle to find new jobs given the changing labour market and skill needs (OECD, 2018[1]). Consequently, automation could aggravate existing socio-economic inequalities by leading to lower wages for some jobs and further job polarisation across types of skills (Acemoglu and Autor, 2011[2]).

Across the OECD, about 46% of jobs face risks of automation. Around 14% of jobs are highly automatable (i.e. face a probability of automation of over 70%). Another 32% of jobs face a significant risk of being strongly affected by automation, which means they are likely to see significant change in their tasks and the required skill sets for such tasks. On average, automation tends to have smaller metropolitan areas in the OECD due to their stronger focus on service-sector jobs. However, several metropolitan areas in Spain, Italy, or Germany, face an even higher automation risk to jobs than the OECD average (Figure 3.1).

The risk of job automation affects almost every second job in Berlin. Compared to other major OECD metropolitan areas, Berlin faces relatively high risks of automation (Figure 3.1). In total, 14% of jobs in Berlin are highly automatable and a further 33% are likely to be changed significantly by automation (see Box 3.1 for a detailed explanation of the computation of risks of automation). Among peer metropolitan areas, only Barcelona, Madrid, Milan and Hamburg record a higher share of jobs that are likely to be automated or significantly transformed. At the other end of the spectrum, the labour markets in Oslo and London appear more resilient with respect to the impact of automation, which will only affect around 28% and 29% of jobs respectively.

Figure 3.1. Almost every second job in Berlin faces risks of automation

Share of jobs at significant and high risk of automation, Berlin and selected peers, 2018

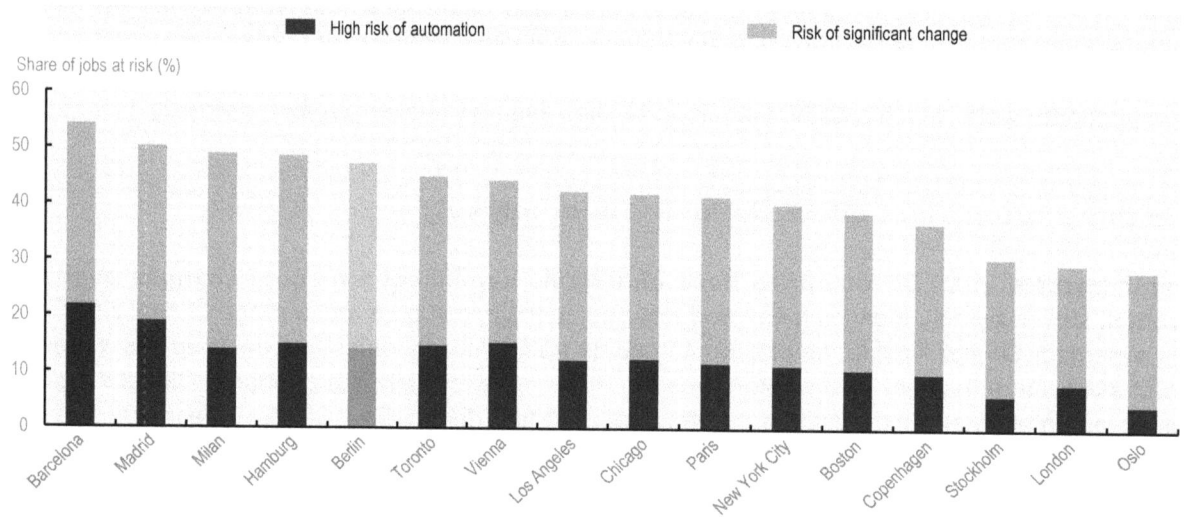

Note: The metropolitan regions show the corresponding TL2 regions. 'High risk of automation' refers to the share of workers featuring a risk of automation of 70% or above. 'Significant risk of change' reflects the share of workers with a risk of automation between 50% and 70%.
Source: OECD Calculations on EU-LFS and Census data.

Box 3.1. Estimating the risk of automation across OECD countries and metropolitan areas

Frey and Osborne (2017[3]) (FO) estimated the number of occupations at high risk of automation in the United States using a two-step methodology. They conducted a workshop with a group of experts in machine learning, whom they provided with a list of 70 occupations and their corresponding O*NET1 task descriptions. Experts were asked "Can the tasks of this job be sufficiently specified, conditional on the availability of big data, to be performed by state of the art computer-controlled equipment?". This allowed for the coding of each occupation as automatable or non-automatable. FO then used a machine learning algorithm to find out more about the links between the coding to automate and the list of O*NET variables. They were able to identify those variables (and their associated bottlenecks) with higher prediction power. High scores on these bottlenecks are likely to mean that an occupation is safe from automation. They could then compute a "probability of computerisation" for each occupation in the US, leading to the aggregate estimate that 47% of US jobs have a probability of automation of more than 70%.

Table 3.1. Automation bottlenecks

Computerisation bottleneck	O*NET variable
Perception and Manipulation	Finger dexterity Manual dexterity Cramped workspace; awkward positions
Creative intelligence	Originality Fine arts
Social intelligence	Social perceptiveness Negotiation Persuasion Assisting and caring for others

Note: Refer to Frey and Osborne (2017[3]) for further details on the definition of automation bottlenecks.
Source: to Frey and Osborne (2017[3]), *The Future of Employment: How Susceptible are Jobs to Computerisation?*.

Building on this approach, Nedelkoska and Quintini (2018[4]) (NQ) calculated the risk of automation across 32 OECD countries. The approach is based on individual-level data from the OECD Survey of Adult Skills (PIAAC), providing information on the skills composition of each person's job and their skillset. While drawing on FO, this methodology presents four main differences: (i) training data in the NQ model is taken from Canada to exploit the country's large sample in PIAAC; (ii) O*NET occupational data for FO's 70 original occupations were manually recoded into the International Standard Classification of Occupations (ISCO); (iii) NQ uses a logistic regression compared to FO's Gaussian process classifier; (iv) NQ found equivalents in PIAAC to match FO's bottlenecks. PIAAC includes variables addressing the bottlenecks identified by FO, but no perfect match exists for each variable. No question in PIAAC could be identified to account for job elements related to "assisting and caring for others", related to occupations in health and social services. This implies that risks of automation based on NQ could be slightly overestimated.

Table 3.2. Automation bottleneck correspondence

FO computerisation bottleneck	PIAAC variable
Perception and Manipulation	Finger dexterity
Creative intelligence	Problem solving (simple) Problem solving (complex)
Social intelligence	Teaching Advising Planning for others Communication Negotiation Influence Sales

Note: Please refer to the source below for further details on the definition of the PIAAC variables.
Source: Nedelkoska and Quintini (2018[4]), "Automation, Skills Use and Training", OECD Social, Employment and Migration Working Papers, No. 202.

Recent studies have pointed out the difficulty in predicting the risk of automation, as different models and variables come into play. Frey and Osborne's original examination of the impact of automation on jobs was focused on machine learning and mobile robotics, but these are not the only key technological developments likely to impact the future of skills. Others have identified the rise of various forms of telepresence and virtual/augmented/mixed forms of reality, as well as the expansion of digital platforms as trends that will have important impacts on the future. The inherent unpredictability of technological progress means that within the growing literature, estimates of the jobs at risk of automation can vary widely, and the timeframes within which these impacts are predicted to occur are similarly broad, ranging from 10 to 50 years. Both the shape disruption will take, and its extent, are uncertain. What is certain is that workers will need to learn new skills and develop new competencies to adapt to changes are on their way (Crawford Urban and Johal, 2020[5]).

Source: Based on OECD (2020[6]), *Preparing for the Future of Work in Canada*.

Across German states, Berlin records the lowest share of jobs at risk of automation. In Berlin, the share of jobs at high risk of automation and the share of jobs that will be significantly changed are both lower than in any other German state (Figure 3.2). However, they are still above the OECD average. Jobs in Thüringen and Mecklenburg-Vorpommern face the highest risks of automation, with more than 50% of jobs facing either high automation risk or risk of significant change. Overall, automation risks are greater in German states than in the OECD, partly due to the greater share of jobs in manufacturing in Germany.

Figure 3.2. Automation risks are greater in the rest of Germany than in Berlin

Percentage of jobs at significant and high risk of automation across Germany, 2020

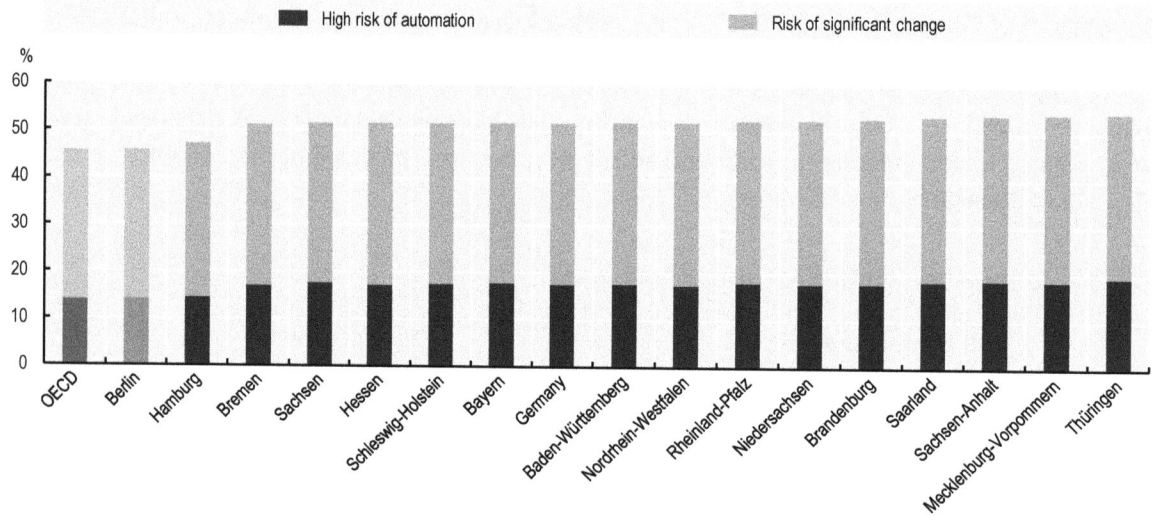

Note: "High risk of automation" refers to the share of workers facing a risk of automation of 70% or more. "Risk of significant change" refers to the share of workers facing a risk of automation between 50% and less than 70%. The OECD average estimates are from Nedelkoska and Quintini (2018).
Source: OECD calculations on EU-LFS data.

The occupational profile of local labour markets help explain why the risk of automation differs within Germany and across OECD metropolitan areas. Occupational differences mainly reflect different industrial structures of regions or metropolitan areas. For example, sectors such as agriculture, construction, food and beverage services, manufacturing, or transport have a higher probability of losing jobs to automation (Box 3.1). German regions that face a higher risk of automation than Berlin tend to rely more strongly on employment in such sectors. Almost 60% of employees in Berlin work in a sector with low automation risks, whereas only around 38% work in high-risk sectors (Figure 3.3). In contrast, in Thüringen, the share of employees in industries with high automation risks amounts to 25%, while only 40% of employees work in industries with low automation risks. Employees in Berlin face lower risks of automation because many work in occupations and industries that involver fewer routine tasks, including jobs in professional and scientific services, finance, or real estate.

Figure 3.3. Berlin has the largest share of employment in industries at low risk of automation in Germany

Employment shares in industries with the lowest and highest risk of automation across Germany, 2019

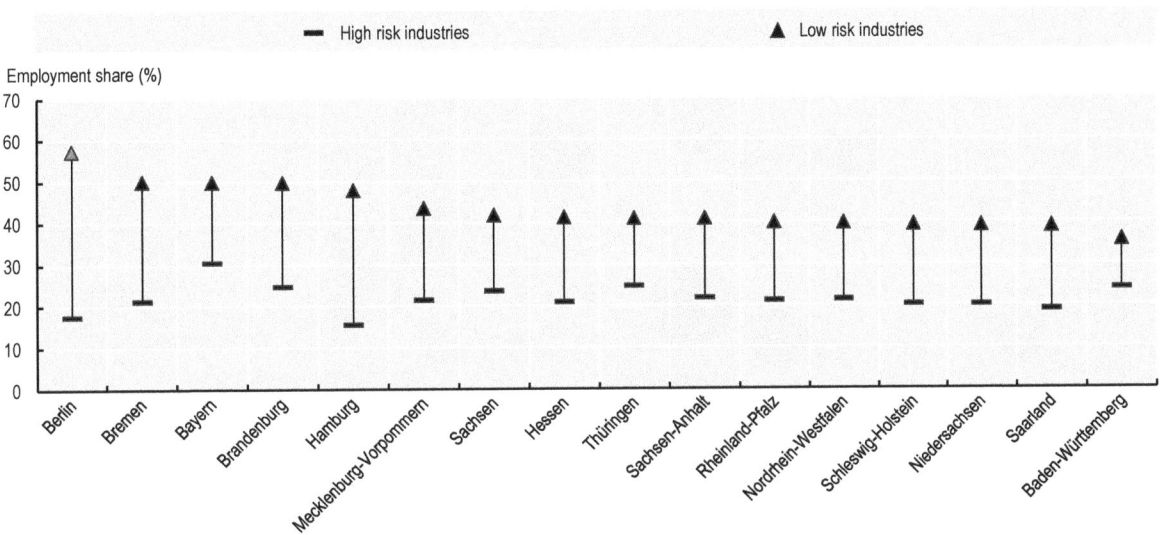

Note: The figure shows the employment shares in the 20 industries with highest average risk of automation (high risk industries) and the 20 industries with lowest average risk of automation (low risk industries). Industries are classified according to 3-digit ISIC Rev. 4. Automation risks are presented in Nedelkoska and Quintini (2018). The figure includes economic activities from ISIC Rev. 4 codes A to J, L to N, and S95.
Source: SBS data by NUTS 2 regions and NACE Rev. 2, Eurostat; Statistics Germany Table 13311-0002.

Promisingly, the bulk of recent job creation in Berlin has mostly taken place in occupations with a low to medium risk of automation. Since 2011, the vast majority of new jobs appeared in high skill occupations that are less vulnerable to automation (Figure 3.4). For example, the number of jobs for information and communication technology professionals increased by around 70 000. Similarly, Berlin's economy created 55 000 jobs for teaching professionals, which consist of occupations that are not only high skilled but also face a relatively low risk of automation. Encouragingly, those low skill occupations that are more robust in light of automation, such as personal service workers, fared better than low skill occupations that are highly vulnerable. The recent patterns of job creation help reduce the exposure of Berlin's labour to the risk of automation. However, the data on job creation also reveal that the opportunities for the low skilled are shrinking, as little to no growth in employment occurred in occupations that provide employment for people with low levels of educations.

Figure 3.4. The majority of newly created jobs in Berlin are in high-skilled occupations with lower automation risks

Job creation compared to risk of automation in Berlin, 2011 to 2020

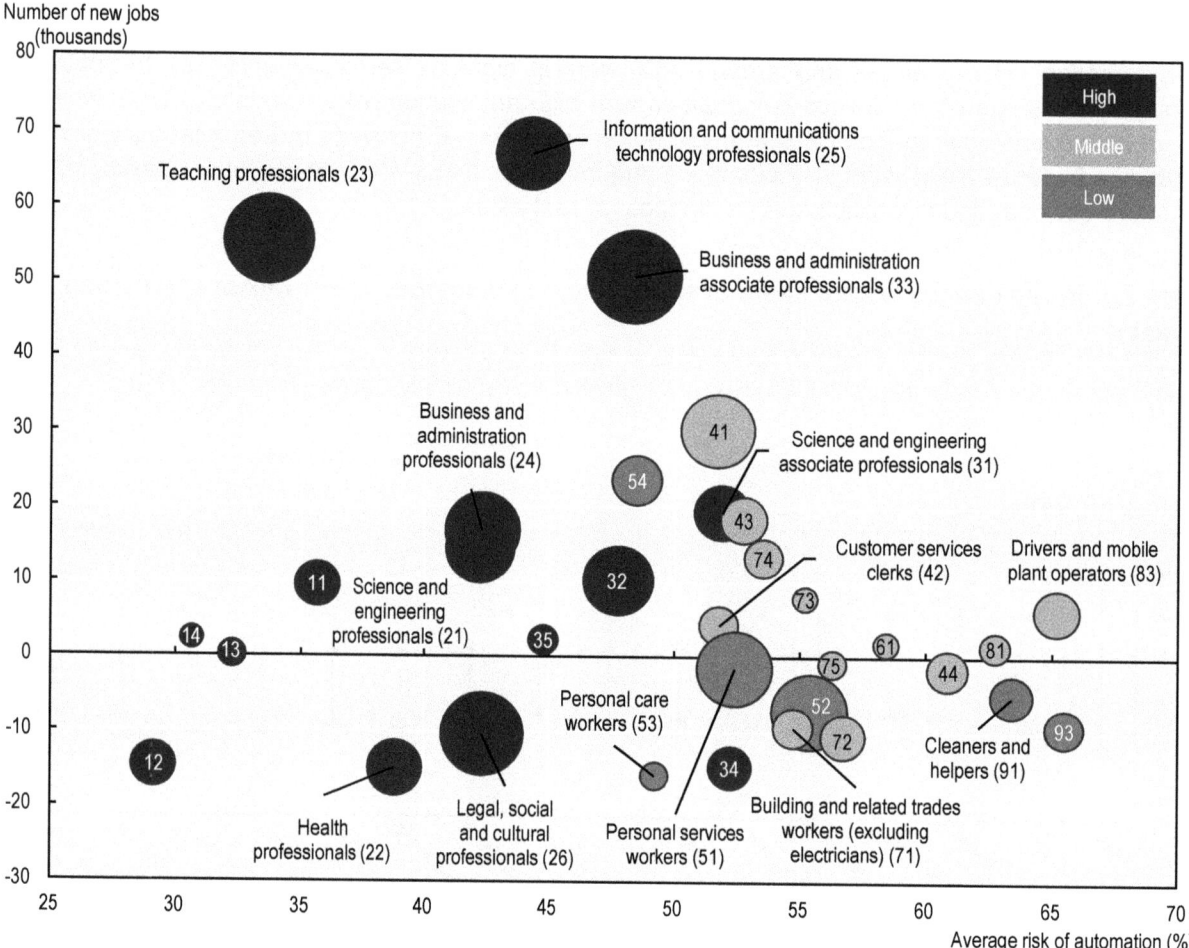

Note: The change in number of jobs (in thousands) is calculated between 2011 and 2020. Occupations (ISCO-08 code indicated in the bubble) are ranked from low to high risk of automation along the horizontal axis. Changes in the number of jobs for each occupation are reported along the vertical axis. The size of the bubble represents the relative share of occupations in Berlin, in 2020.
Source: OECD calculations on EU-LFS data.

Box 3.2. Which industries have the highest risk of automation?

The following table presents the 20 industries at highest average risk of automation and the 20 industries at lowest risk. The industries with high risk of automation belong mostly to the primary and the secondary sector. Few service industries face a high risk of automation, though exceptions include food and beverage services, land transport, waste collection and treatment, and services to buildings and landscape. In contrast, almost all industries with relatively low probability of automation belong to the service sector.

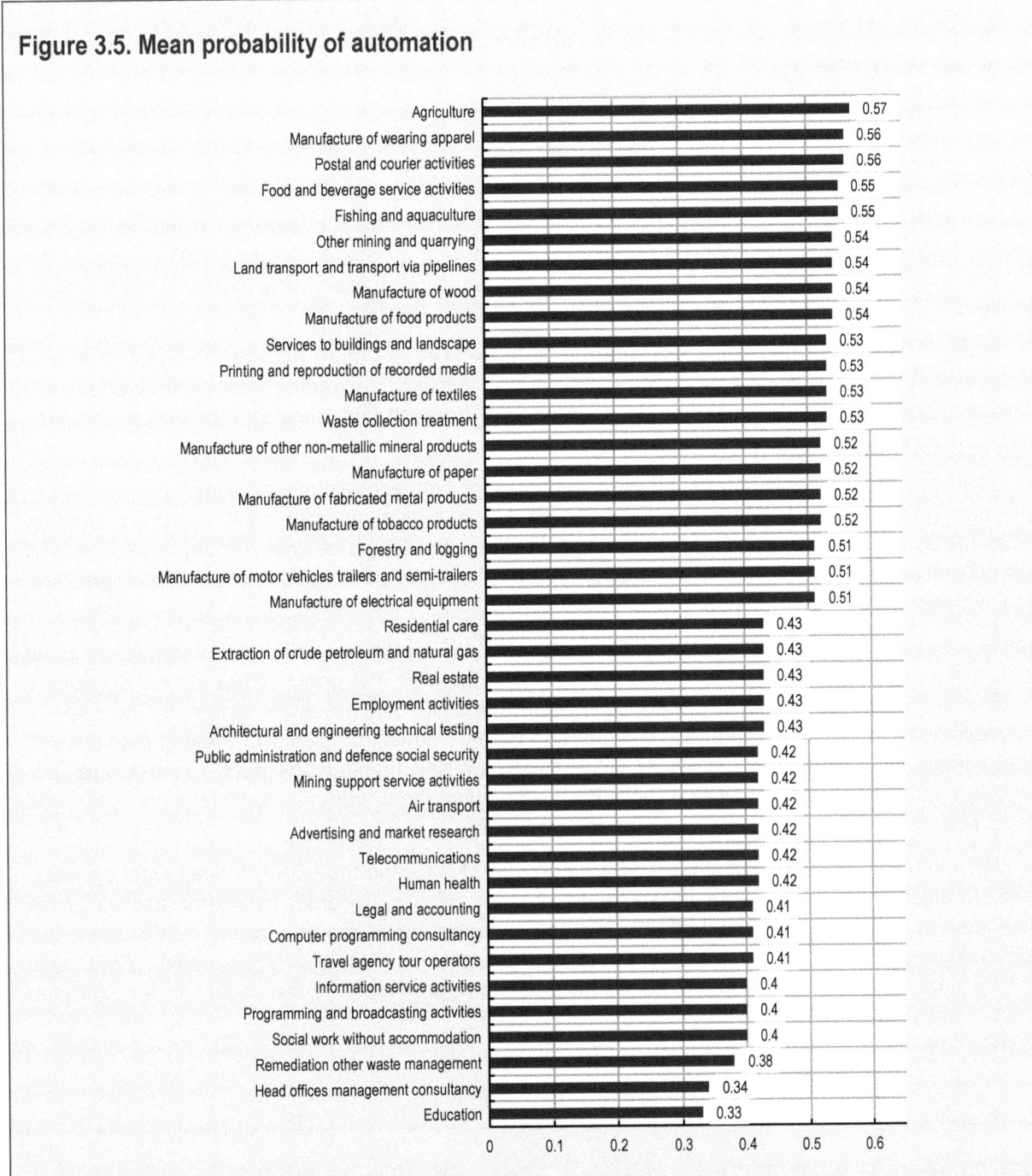

Figure 3.5. Mean probability of automation

Note: The figure only includes the 20 industries with highest average risk of automation and the 20 industries with lowest average risk of automation. The classification is ISIC Rev. 4, 2-digit.
Source: Survey of Adult Skills (PIAAC) 2012, 2015; Nedelkoska and Quintini (2018[4]), *Automation, skills use and training*.

Automation and digitalisation make digital skills ever more relevant in Berlin. Digital skills are essential for people to maximise their opportunities, work efficiently in a job; and are crucial for ensuring productivity and growth in Berlin. Digital skills are particularly important for those groups that are most at risk of redundancy because new jobs increasingly require basic or advanced digital skills and the ability to work in a technology-rich environment. To enhance employability of vulnerable groups in the labour market,

Berlin could look at interesting local initiatives such as the Local Digital Skills Partnership in Lancashire in the UK that aim to equip workers with highly sought after digital skills in close collaboration with the local business community (Box 3.3).

> ### Box 3.3. Lancashire Digital Skills Partnership, UK
>
> The Lancashire Digital Skills Partnership (LDSP) seeks to improve Lancashire's digital skills in an inclusive way by bringing together public, private and non-profit stakeholders. LDSP is part of the Lancashire Enterprise Partnership's Skills and Employment Hub (LEP) and was formed in collaboration with the UK Department for Digital, Culture, Media and Sport (DCMS).
>
> The strategic framework has four key themes: Future Workforce (future pipeline of digital skills and talent), Skilled and Productive Workforce (digital skills in the workplace and for technology adoption), Inclusive Workforce (digital inclusion), and an Informed Approach (influence and inform Lancashire's priorities in employment and skills).
>
> The LDSP provided suggestions based on an analysis of Lancashire's digital landscape, defined in eight main pillars of activity: Careers education; equality and diversity; curriculum design; promoting Lancashire as a place to live and work in the digital sector; developing businesses' digital skills; digital apprenticeships; coherence across the digital strategies of local authorities and other partners; and digital inclusion.
>
> Despite some issues with recruiting in the digital industry, e.g. a high rate of skills shortage opening, its substantial predicted development makes it a key area for the LEP. The goal is to assist local employers in finding candidates for hard-to-fill positions in specialised digital skill areas and to support job seekers with guaranteed interviews. The LDSP designs and creates new strategies and training packages in digital sectors with skills needs, together with businesses and training providers. For example, the intensive and flexible (up to 16 weeks) Skills Bootcamps give the opportunity to develop skills needed in local sectors guaranteeing interviews after the Bootcamp.
>
> The joint venture Fast Track Digital Work Force Fund, by DCMS and the LDSP, funded eight projects, related to digital marketing, robots, data science or cyber-security, in order to provide access to the digital industry to underrepresented participants and encourage diversity and inclusion. Moreover, the LDSP has developed relationships with business partners, such as Google, AWS, openSAP, the Lloyds Banking Group or Freeformers to provide further training opportunities to the county in, for example, coding or big data.
>
> Source: OECD (2021[7]), *Future-Proofing Adult Learning in London, UK*.

Labour markets in the OECD are polarising, partly reflecting a shift in labour supply

Even before the COVID-19 pandemic started, most OECD economies experienced dramatic shifts in their labour markets. Over the last decades, labour markets across the OECD have become increasingly polarised. The share of employment in middle-skill jobs has declined strongly relative to jobs with higher or lower skill levels (OECD, 2017[8]). High-skill jobs include managers, professionals and technicians; middle-skill jobs compose clerks, craft and related trades workers, machine operators and assemblers; and low-skill jobs include elementary occupations, service workers, and shop and market sales workers. In almost all OECD countries, job polarisation has been characterised primarily by a shift towards high-skill occupations (OECD, 2019[9]).

Job polarisation is not only part of labour market transformations but also poses a social challenge in OECD societies. It raises public concern about growing inequality in OECD countries. Middle-skill jobs were historically associated with a middle-class lifestyle and socio-economic mobility for future generations. In recent years, however, the overall skill distribution on the labour market has shifted towards higher-skill jobs as growth in high-skill occupations has outpaced growth in middle- and low-skill occupations, which has changed the relationship between skills and income classes. Consequently, middle-skill workers are now more likely to be in lower-income classes than middle-income classes (OECD, 2019[9]). Furthermore, the wage structure in many OECD countries is now also showing a growing divide between top earners and others, instead of experiencing growth at both ends of the wage structure.

Skills-biased technological change has been driving a labour market polarisation across the OECD. This is particularly noticeable in large cities, which tend to be at the forefront of labour market transformations. Across OECD metropolitan areas, labour markets are increasingly polarising into high and low skilled jobs. In contrast, middle-skill jobs are rapidly disappearing in many places. All the 17 OECD metropolitan areas considered, including Berlin, have lost middle-skill jobs in relative terms since 2000 (Figure 3.6). On average, the share of workers in such jobs decreased by more than 7 percentage points between 2000 and 2018. Most of those metropolitan areas have replaced middle-skill jobs with both high-skill and low-skill jobs, with the former recording the largest relative increase in jobs. In fact, 16 metropolitan areas have mostly replaced middle-skill jobs with high-skill jobs.

Figure 3.6. Job polarisation in Berlin is less pronounced than in most other OECD metropolitan areas

Change in the share of employment for high skill, middle skill and low skill jobs in Berlin and selected peers, 2000-18

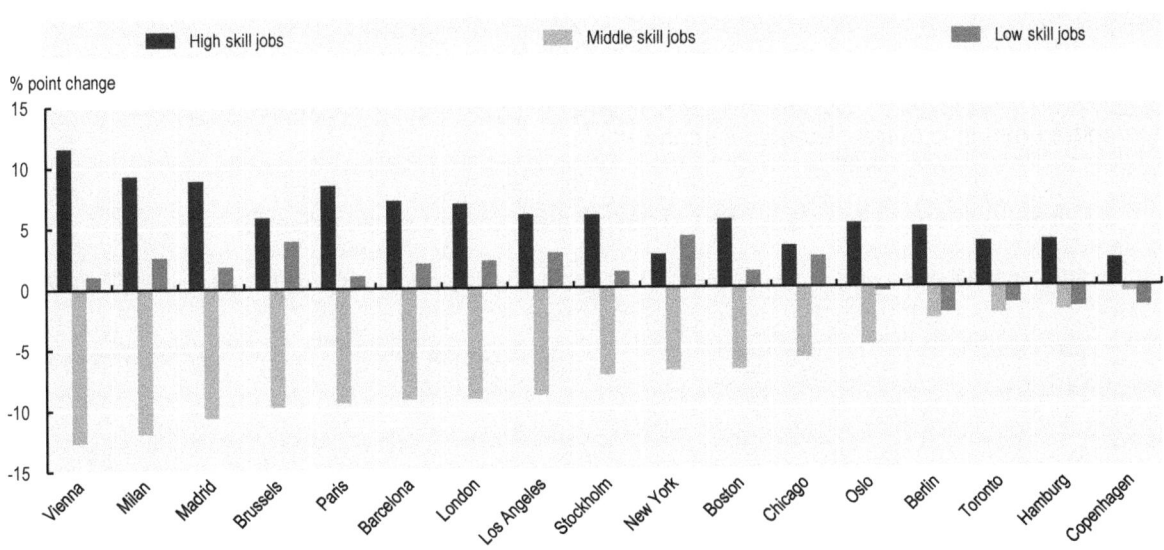

Note: The data correspond to the TL2 regions that compose the respective metropolitan area.
Source: OECD calculations on Labour Force Surveys.

Compared to other OECD metropolitan areas, middle-skilled jobs disappeared at a lower rate in Berlin. Since 2000, the share of middle-skilled jobs fell by 2.7 percentage points (Figure 3.6). A significant rise in high-skilled jobs (+ 4.9 percentage points) more than compensated for the loss in middle-skilled jobs. Contrary to most comparable OECD metropolitan areas, Berlin did not experience a simultaneous increase in the share of low-skilled jobs. Instead, the share of low-skilled jobs fell by 2.2 percentage points. In summary, Berlin's labour market has experienced a shift towards high-skilled jobs, with both middle-skilled and low-skilled jobs falling at similar rates.[1]

The green transition: an opportunity for Berlin?

The green transition to a low-carbon economy is another major development that will shape labour markets over the coming decades. Reaching the political objective of reducing emissions and achieving a net-zero economy, requires decisive actions by many countries around the world. Those actions, which include the phasing out of fossil fuels and a move towards renewable energies, will inevitably also affect the labour market. Jobs and sectors that support the green transition could thrive, while others that are emission-intensive such as the chemical industry or parts of manufacturing could see job losses or at least a significant structural transformation.

The opportunities and challenges that the green transition brings will differ vastly across local labour markets. Due to differences in their economic structure and the share of jobs across sectors, some local labour markets will face significant risks while others could benefit from growing green sectors. Currently, a lack of clear empirical evidence on green jobs and skills across local areas hampers the assessment of where the green transition might create new economic opportunities other than in the renewable energy sector. However, by looking at a subset of jobs that are emission-intensive, one can assess the extent to which jobs across OECD regions might be put at risk by a move towards net-zero economy.

In Berlin, employment risks due to the net-zero transition appear low. Figure 3.7 presents data on the share of jobs in four manufacturing sectors that entail, on average, high levels of emissions. Those sectors are transport, coal and other mining, chemical and plastic products, and other manufacturing. In Berlin, these sectors only account for around 0.8% of total employment, the lowest share across all German federal states. Similarly, the share of employment in those sectors is much lower that the OECD average of 2.2%. In the extent to which those jobs could be classified as "brown jobs" that face heightened risk from the move to a net-zero economy, Berlin's labour market seems relatively well-shielded. The relevant dominance of the service sector in Berlin's economy provides further protection against adverse shocks from the green transition, as the major impact is likely to be on manufacturing jobs. Looking a step further, the green transition could in fact provide new economic opportunities for Berlin supported by its young workforce and dynamic entrepreneurship scene.

Figure 3.7. Employment risks due to the net-zero transition are small in Berlin

Percent of total regional employment in industries at risk due to the net-zero transition, large regions (TL2), 2017

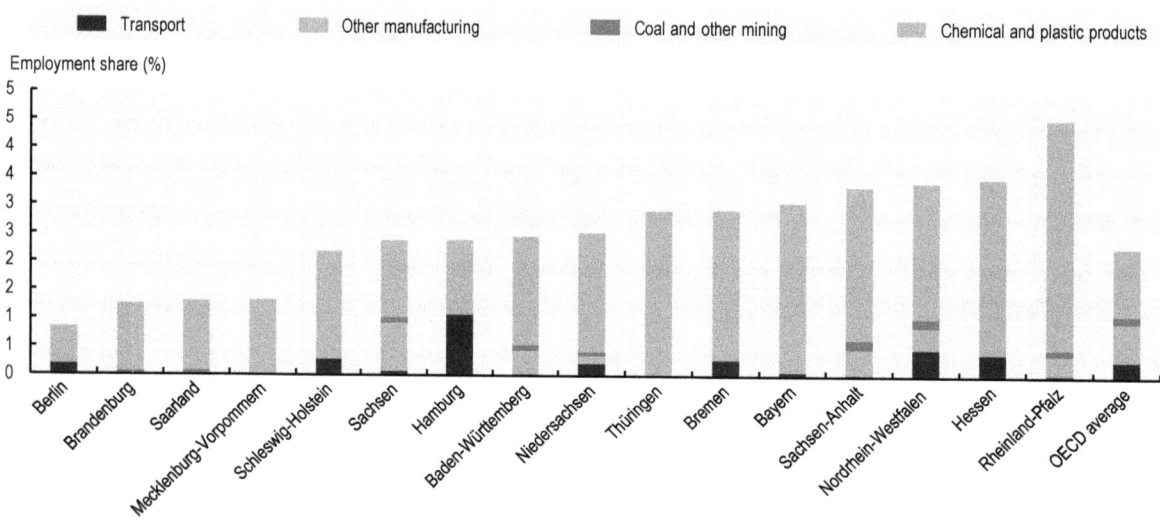

Note: The y-axis shows the employment share in industries put at risk until 2040. For details on the methodology, see OECD (2021, p. 106[10]).
Source: OECD estimates based on EU-LFS data.

> **Box 3.4. Assessing employment risks due to the-zero transition**
>
> The dynamic general equilibrium model OECD ENV-Linkages allows illustrating economic impacts of climate mitigation policy scenarios several decades into the future, linking activity and employment to GHG emissions (Château, Dellink and Lanzi, 2014[11]). Building on this model and applying it to large OECD regions, OECD analysis identifies regional employment risks across sectors under the goals of the Paris Climate Agreement (OECD, 2021[10]).
>
> Overall, the two-digit ISIC sectors identified as being at risk of employment losses due to the net-zero carbon transition include: Mining of coal and lignite; Other mining and quarrying; Manufacture of textiles; Manufacture of coke and refined petroleum products; Manufacture of chemicals and chemical products; Manufacture of rubber and plastics products; Manufacture of other transport equipment; Water transport; Air transport. The petrochemical sectors contain most of the employment in sectors likely at risk of employment losses due to the net-zero carbon transition in OECD and partner countries: 32% of employment in sectors at risk is employed in the manufacture of rubber and plastics products and 20% is employed in the manufacture of chemicals and chemical products.
>
> Source: OECD (2021[10]), *OECD Regional Outlook 2021*.

Changing skills needs in Berlin

The transformation of the world of work changes the skills firms need. As a result, it could create a discrepancy between the demand for skills and its supply, which is based on the education and the qualifications of the labour force. Since skills and their effective use are a fundamental driver of economic development and productivity, rising skills mismatches and gaps could harm Berlin's economic prosperity and growth. Across the OECD, skills gaps help explain a significant share of cross-country variation in labour productivity (Adalet McGowan and Andrews, 2017[12]). Industry-level analysis shows that firms in industries with higher skills mismatches tend to have a lower labour productivity performance (Adalet McGowan and Andrews, 2015[13]). Crucially, skills also matter for resilience, as they allow workers to be more flexible in reacting to changing labour markets and economic crises.

The matching of workers to jobs in which they can utilise their skills in the best possible way is a vital element of functioning labour markets. To the contrary, mismatches between workers' skills and the requirements of their jobs can have negative effects, ranging from lower job satisfaction, wages, and labour productivity to unused potential of human capital (OECD, 2018[1]). Mismatch by qualification is one source of such skills mismatches. It arises when workers' educational attainment is above (over-qualification) or below (under-qualification) the level usually required by the tasks of their job.

Skills mismatches by qualification are widespread in Berlin. Around 41% of all workers in Berlin have a job that does not correspond to their level of qualification (Figure 3.8). Twenty-two percent of workers in Berlin have a job for which they are formally overqualified. Another 19% appear to be underqualified for their job, meaning they do not have the skills and qualifications normally expected to fill out their position. Compared to selected large and economically important OECD metropolitan areas, Berlin records the second highest (out of 13) degree of skills mismatch by qualification, pointing out the strong disconnect between labour supply and demand in the local economy. This is particularly true for the over-qualification of workers, i.e. people working below their educational attainment, which exceeds the OECD and EU averages of 17% and 13% significantly.

Skills gaps and mismatches already inhibit Berlin's economy. With the rapidly changing demand for new skills and the emergence of new types of jobs, the problem could become more severe if it is not addressed. Therefore, it is more important than ever to have a robust adult education and training system that provides on- and off-ramps for all individuals and firms to participate. Such a system will allow workers to gain new skills, retrain, or extend existing skills in bringing them up-to-date with recent developments. An important prerequisite for dealing with and alleviating skills gaps and mismatches consists of collecting sound data on the local labour market. A number of publicly available tools provide such data that policy makers can use to track regional labour demand, which helps design effective policy (Figure 3.5).

Figure 3.8. More than 40% of workers in Berlin are mismatched by level of qualification

Percentage of workers across metropolitans occupying jobs that do not match their educational attainment, 2018

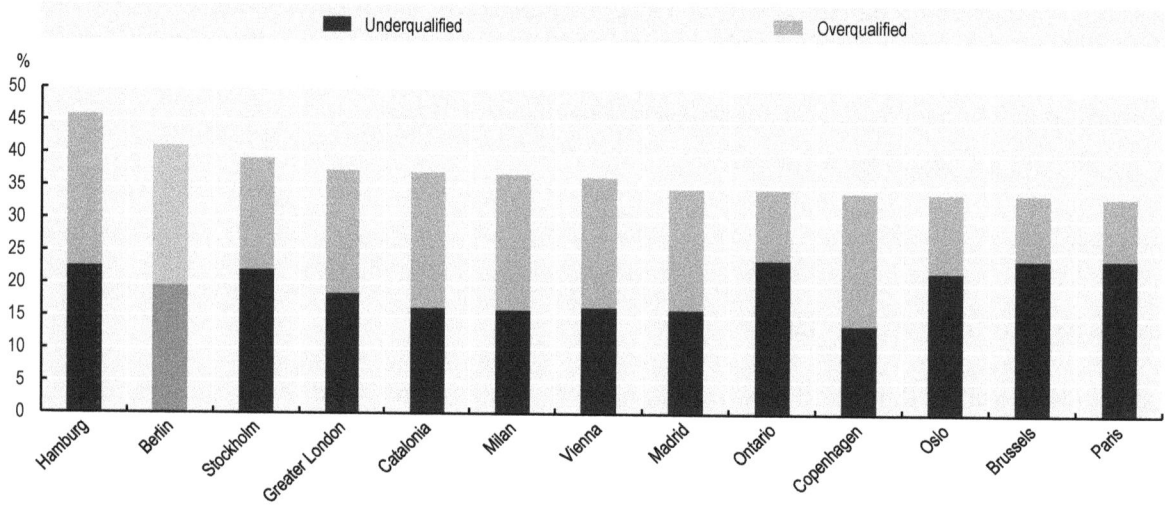

Note: ISCED groups 0-2, 3, 4, 5-8. For Canada, ISCED groups 0-2, 3, 4, 5-6. ISCED groups 302, 303 and 304 are considered to be 3 according to the newest 2011 ISCED classification.
Source: OECD calculations on European labour force survey 2018 and Calculations based on Stats Canada Census 2016.

Box 3.5. Tools used by the Federal Employment Agency to analyse regional labour demand in Berlin

The German *Bundesagentur für Arbeit* ("Federal Employment Agency") offers a range of publicly available tools that allow tracking regional labour demand by profession:

Fachkräfteradar: The tool monitors the ratio of vacancies and unemployment for a large range of occupations across German federal states and labour market regions.[2]

Fachkräftebedarfe: An interactive tool that presents diagrams and tables on key statistics on labour market shortages for different occupations by federal state, labour market regions and districts (Kreise).[3]

Engpassanalyse: The tool presents indicators on labour market shortages for different occupations and occupational groups across different areas in Germany. For each occupation/occupational group, the tool shows a composite labour market tightness measure that is based on six indicators: the time to fill a vacancy, the ratio of unemployed to vacancies, occupation specific unemployment rates, the change in foreigners as a share of all employed in those occupations who are liable to social security contributions, the exit rate from unemployment in a given occupation, and the change in median salary.[4]

Entgeltatlas: The tool provides information on average salaries by occupation in German federal states and a range of larger cities.[5]

Non-standard work is on the rise in Berlin

Many labour markets across the OECD have undergone a gradual transition away from traditional open-ended contracts. Non-standard forms of work, which include temporary, part-time, or self-employed work, have been rising (see Box 3.6 for information on the definition of non-standard work). Changing consumer preferences and new technological developments are two important factors explaining the increase in non-standard work forms. The latter allows firms to adopt more job flexibility and outsourcing of tasks, including the hiring of temporary help or freelance contractors. The former, have caused a shift among firms to more just-in-time delivery and customised services.

Box 3.6. Defining non-standard work

Non-standard work (NSW) arrangements are defined by what they are not: full-time dependent employment with a contract of indefinite duration – or what is generally considered the "standard" work arrangement. NSW therefore includes:

- Temporary workers - workers in fixed-term contracts, including casual employees (duration is not fixed, but hours can vary), and seasonal workers;
- Part-time workers;
- The self-employed.

While this definition may be considered problematic – as it lumps together precarious and non-precarious forms of work – the convention is followed by a large part of academic research as well as by international organisations. For this reason, this chapter adopts this definition.

An additional challenge lies in the fact that the distinction between different forms of employment has become increasingly intricate. In particular, there is a growing grey area between self-employment and wage employment. The growing numbers of self-employed working for just one company represent a group on the border between two categories. While these blurred lines are at the heart of the current debate on the benefits and downsides of the gig economy, data that allows researchers to settle the debate is scarce

Source: OECD (2018[14]), *Job Creation and Local Economic Development 2018: Preparing for the Future of Work*, OECD Publishing, Paris, https://dx.doi.org/10.1787/9789264305342-en; OECD (2015[15]), "Non-standard work, job polarisation and inequality", in *In It Together: Why Less Inequality Benefits All*, OECD Publishing, Paris, https://dx.doi.org/10.1787/9789264235120-7-en.

Non-standard work brings new opportunities as well as challenges for local labour markets. It offers opportunities to find employment or increase flexibility for some workers but it also worsens working conditions for others. On the one hand, non-standard work arrangements can enhance the compatibility of work and family life and increase worker flexibility more generally. Thus, it can encourage labour force participation, especially among those who would otherwise have stayed out of the labour market. For instance, it can help women to combine professional and personal responsibilities. Moreover, it can facilitate school-to-work transitions by providing a stepping-stone for young people (OECD, 2018[14]).

However, on the other hand, non-standard work is often associated with worse working conditions in terms of reduced job security, higher income volatility, and slower career progression.

Non-standard work employment has increased in most OECD countries since 2000. Temporary contracts have become more common in OECD countries, especially among young workers (Figure 3.9 Panel A). Compared to 1980, the share of OECD workers under the age of 26 in a fixed-term contract has risen from 17% to 25% in 2016. Moreover, the share of employees in part-time work has also increased significantly (Figure 3.9 Panel B). While a large part of this trend is due to the entry of women into the labour market that historically struggled to combine family and professional life, part-time work has also increased amongst men.

Figure 3.9. Non-standard employment has been rising across OECD countries

Share of temporary and part-time work, OECD countries, 2000-16

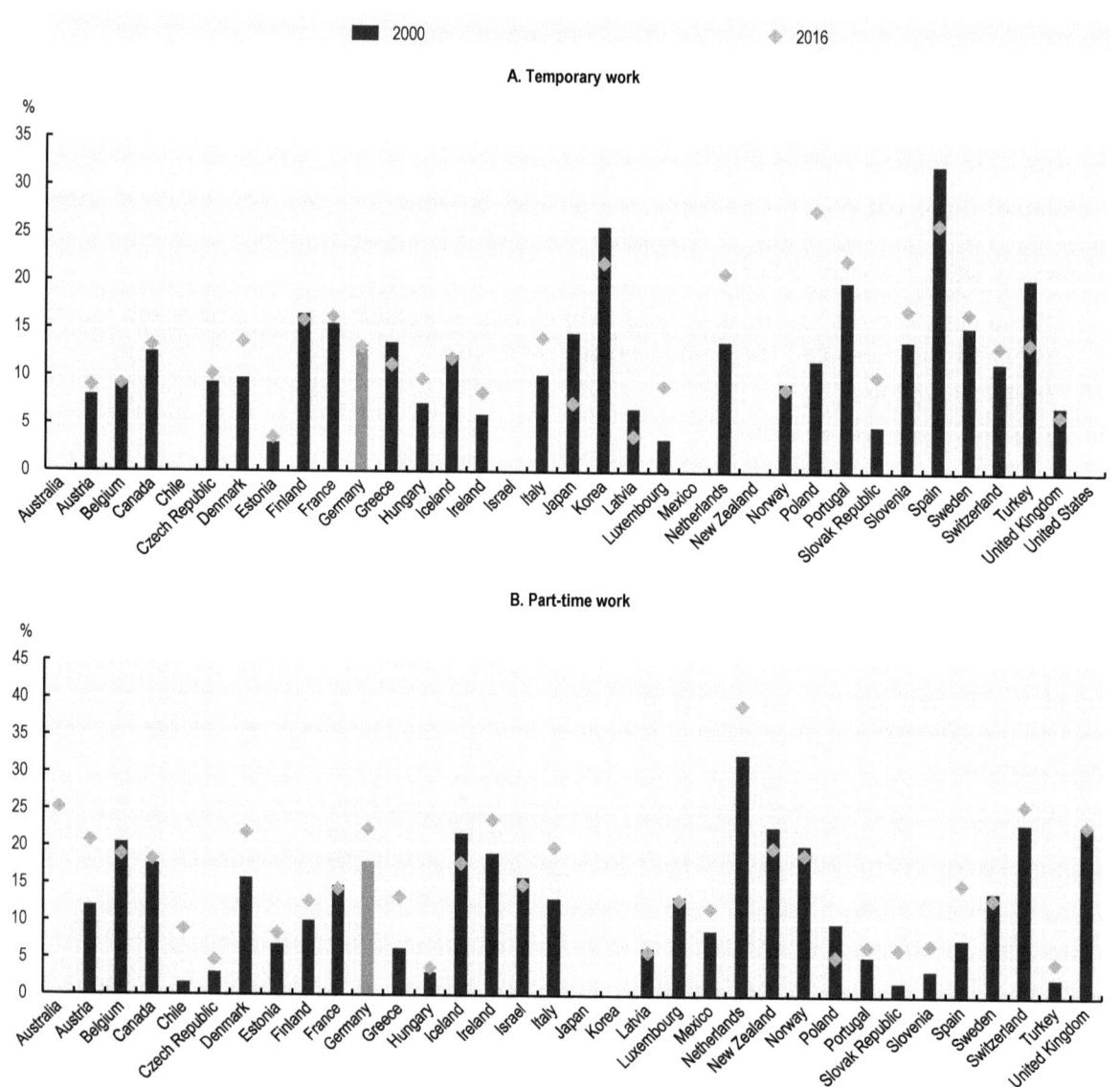

Source: OECD (2018), "Labour Market Statistics: Employment by permanency of the job & Full-time and part-time employment - common definition: incidence", OECD Employment and Labour Market Statistics (database), http://dx.doi.org/10.1787/lfs-data-en.

Part-time work has increased in Berlin, Germany and the OECD

In Berlin, part-time employment has grown at a similar pace as Germany overall. In 2019, around 26% of employment in was part time, an increase of 6 percentage points from 2002 (Figure 3.10). In Germany overall, a slightly higher share of total employment, 27%, is part time. Compared to the EU27 countries, part-time employment in Berlin and Germany is relatively high. On average, 18% of 16 to 64 year olds have a part-time job in the EU27. A number of reasons could help explain this difference. For example, women make up a large share of part-time employees. As such, part-time employment can be a means of ensuring a work-life balance and making family and professional life compatible. In countries such as the Netherlands, Switzerland, Germany, the United Kingdom or Norway, women's increased labour market participation partly explains the rise in part-time employment, with women being more than twice as likely as men to work part time and on average, almost one quarter of women – often mothers – work part-time (OECD, 2020[16]). However, part-time employment often comes with disadvantages too.

Figure 3.10. More than a quarter of 16 to 64 year olds in Berlin have part-time work

Share of part-time employment in total employment by federal state, 2002 and 2019, 16 to 64 year olds

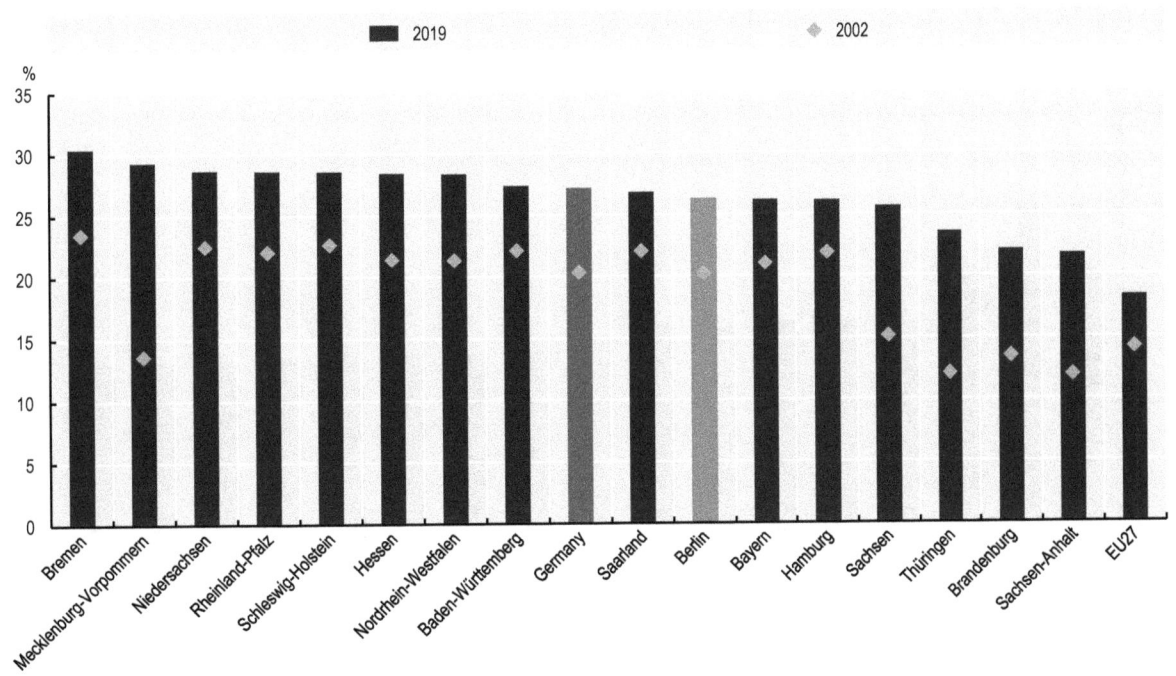

Note: 2002 earliest value available.
Source: Eurostat, table lfst_r_lfe2eftpt.

Part-time employees face higher job security and tend to earn lower hourly wages in OECD countries (OECD, 2018[17]). Poverty rates tend to be higher for part-time workers than for standard employees. While on average 10% of part-time workers live in a household with an annual disposable income of less than 50% of the national median, this is only the case for 3% of standard employees (OECD, 2020[16]). Furthermore, part-time workers are less likely to participate in training, which has a negative impact on their future earnings. Lower training participation also means that part-time workers are less likely to adapt to the future of work and changing skills requirement. As pointed out in the previous section, automation and digitalisation change labour market needs and skill profiles that employers seek. Part-time workers are less able to react to these developments by using learning opportunities to retrain or upskill.

Another dimension of non-standard work is self-employment, which has been increasing significantly in Berlin. More than 13% of all workers in Berlin are self-employed, making it the federal state in Germany with the highest rate of self-employment (Figure 3.11). Self-employment is not only much more common in Berlin than elsewhere in Germany but also grown over the past 15 years, while it fell in Germany overall. The share of self-employed workers grew from around 11.7% to 13.4% between 2004 and 2019 in Berlin, whereas it decreased from 9.8% to 8.5% nationally. As of 2019, the proportion of self-employment among workers in Berlin was similar to the average of the EU27 countries. However, contrary to the development in Berlin's economy, the EU27 self-employment rate markedly decreased from 2004 to 2019. One factor that contributes to the rise of self-employment in Berlin is the emergence of the digital economy. Some self-employed workers in the digital economy have been able to benefit from new markets and opportunities by finding high-value added work as independent professionals or freelancers. However, for others, self-employment in the digital economy takes on precarious forms, as some work for a single client that is effectively their employer, without having the benefits of a formal employer-employee relationship including social security or work regulation that protects employees.

Figure 3.11. Self-employment in Berlin has increased

Changes in self-employment rate across German federal states, 2004 and 2019

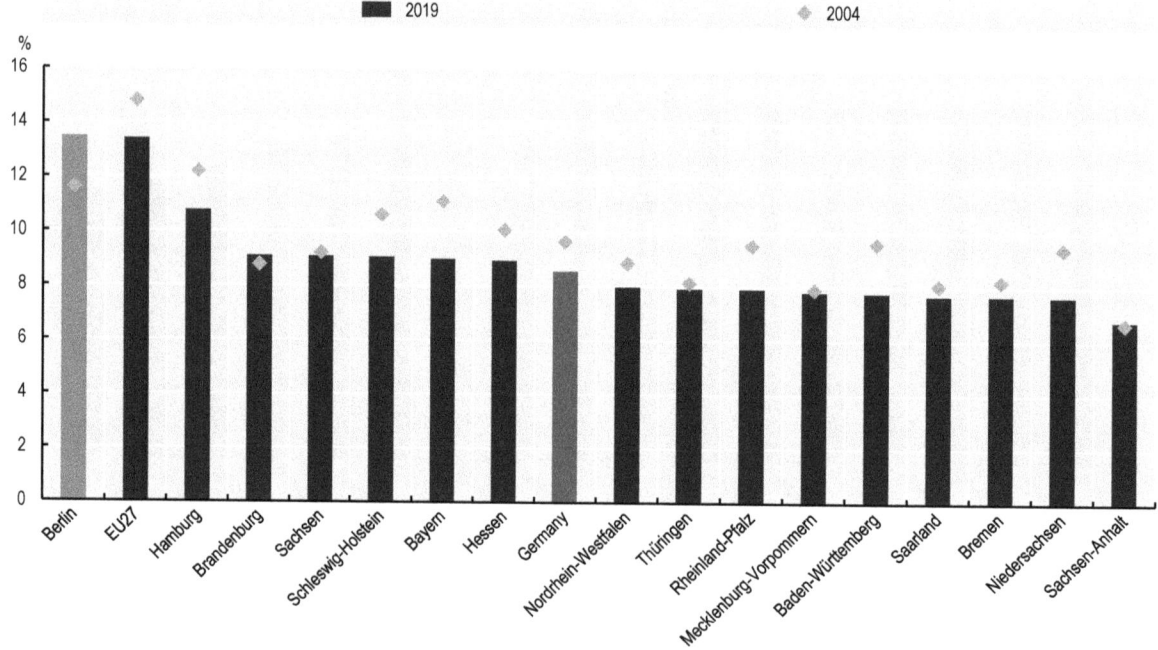

Note: 2004 earliest value available.
Source: Eurostat, table lfst_r_lfe2estat.

COVID-19 and digitalisation lead to surging demand for digital skills

During the COVID-19 pandemic, Berlin has experienced a surge in demand for digital skills. The shift to teleworking has led to the adoption of new technology and a proliferation of technological solutions to work elements such as meetings that were limited by social distancing measures. This push, which has forced firms and workers to experiment with new working arrangements and embrace virtual approaches to some of their tasks, is likely to have a lasting impact. It has emphasised the relevance of being able to work in a digital environment and has thus increased the demand for digital skills.

Berlin has recorded a significant jump in new jobs that require advanced information and communications technology (ICT) skills. From the start of the pandemic until the end of 2020, the share of job postings in Berlin that require advanced ICT skills rose from 26% to 33% (Figure 3.12). Such jobs entail specialised skills such as programming, coding and data analysis (see Box 3.7 for more details). While many German cities saw a rising demand for ICT skills during the pandemic, it rose particularly fast in Berlin, suggesting that Berlin might be experiencing a faster transformation of its local economy than other places in Germany. Looking at the requirements of job postings offers a timely alternative to measuring labour demand and the changing skills mix in Berlin's economy.

Figure 3.12. Labour demand for advanced ICT skills has increased in Berlin during the pandemic

Share of job postings requiring advanced ICT skills, German cities, 2015-20

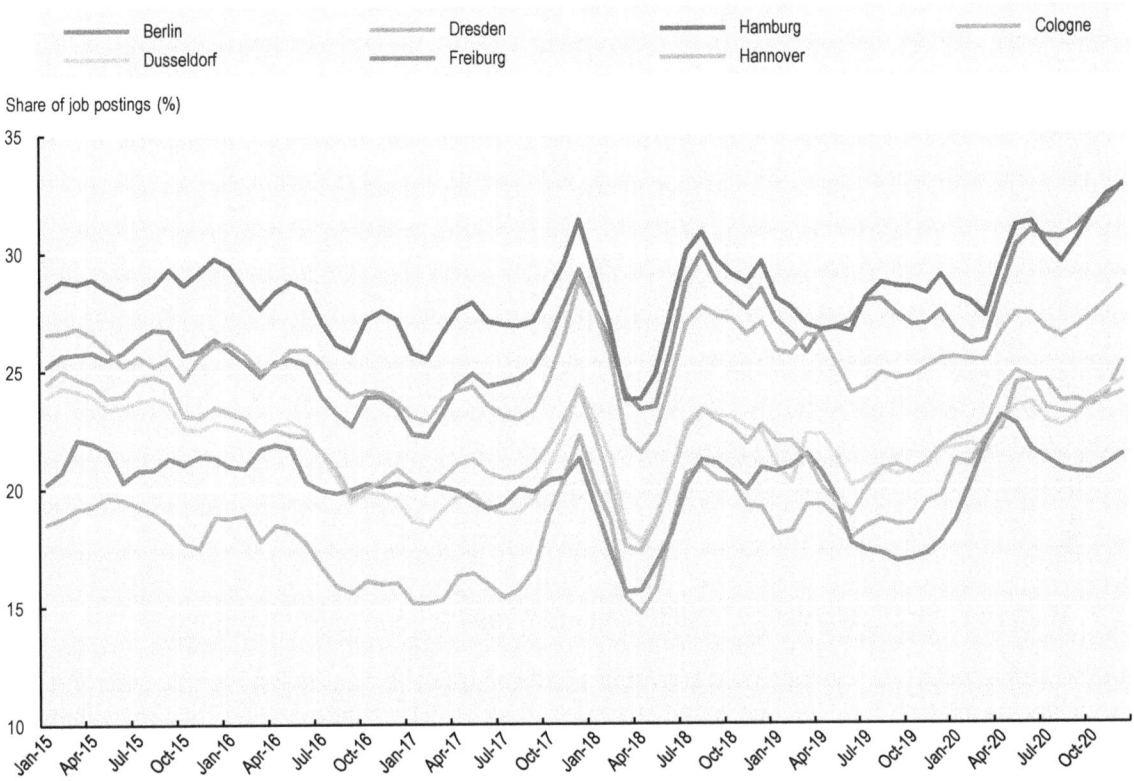

Note: For a description of the methodology applied, see Box 3.7.
Source: OECD calculations using Burning Glass Technology job postings data.

Contrary to advanced digital skills such as programming or data analysis, demand for more basic digital skills has not risen. Not all digital skills recorded significant increases in demand as firms and employees had to embrace digital ways of working. Demand for generic digital skills that encompass simple ICT skills, for instance referring to knowledge of "MS Excel", remained mostly constant (Figure 3.13). In fact, their relative importance has fallen since 2015, which probably indicates that such skills are increasingly taking for granted. They appear to become a minimum work requirement for many jobs in Berlin.

Figure 3.13. Labour demand for generic ICT skills remained unchanged during the pandemic

Share of job postings requiring generic ICT skills, German cities, 2015-20

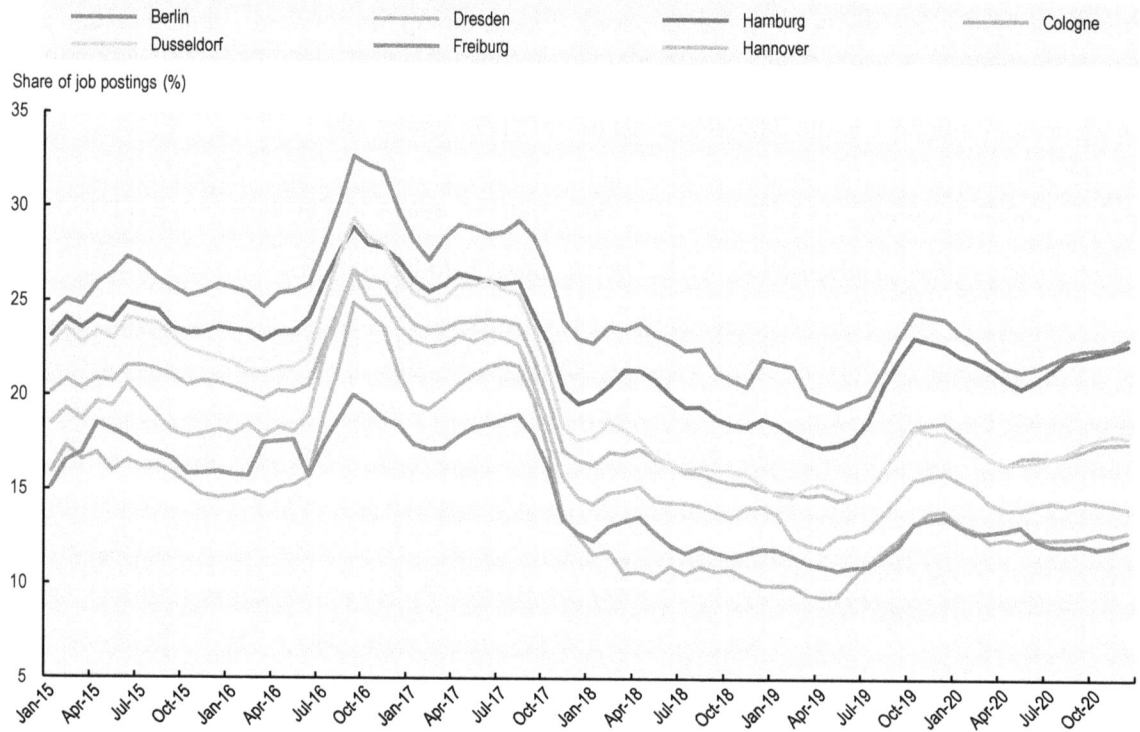

Note: For a description of the methodology applied, see Box 3.7.
Source: OECD calculations using Burning Glass Technology job postings data.

Box 3.7. Methodology to calculate ICT skill demand based on online job postings

The report uses online job postings data provided by Burning Glass Technology to calculate the share of job vacancies that require generic or advanced ICT skills. The methodology follows a three-step procedure. First, the total number of unique monthly job postings is calculated by region. In a second step, the skill requirements listed in each job posting is used to calculate a dummy indicator of "generic" or "advanced" ICT skills for each job, in a procedure closely following previous OECD work on categorising these skills (Brüning and Mangeol, 2020[18]). The classification into generic and advanced skills is intuitive: Generic skills are simple ICT skills captured by key words such as "MS Excel" or "data". Advanced ICT skills are more specialised skills such as programming, coding and data analysis. These skills are captured by key words such as "algorithm" or "data mining" but also indirectly when knowledge of software such as "Python" or "Oracle" is mentioned in the posting. Jobs that require both generic and advanced ICT skills are classified as requiring advanced ICT skills, implicitly making the plausible assumption that generic skills would not suffice to carry out the job.

In a final step, the total numbers of job postings that require generic or advanced ICT skills are summed up by region and divided by the total number of regional job postings calculated in the first step. It should further be noted that from July 2018 onwards, Burning Glass Technology started scraping job postings data using a different methodology as well as different data sources. To make data comparable over a longer period and to avoid structural breaks in the time series, the figures shown in this report

> do not make use of these updated data sources. Thus, other figures on regional online job postings published by the OECD using more recent data over a shorter period may differ slightly from the numbers shown in this report.

Comprehensive data on digital skills among Berlin's workforce are missing but alternative measures can provide an approximation. Ideally, extensive surveys of adult workers or firms could highlight the extent to which individuals have the necessary digital skills to succeed in the local economy. However, most of those data sources are either not representative at the subnational level (e.g. the OECD Programme for the International Assessment of Adult Competencies (PIAAC) or do not offer systematic evidence on digital skills gaps as in the case of employer surveys that cover Berlin. To approximate basic digital skills, regular internet use might offer an alternative. In Berlin, as in other OECD metropolitan areas, internet use has not only risen over the past decade but has become ubiquitous in most people's lives (Figure 3.14).

Figure 3.14. Almost everyone uses the internet regularly in OECD metropolitan areas

Share of population that used the internet at least once over the past 3 months, Berlin and selected peers, 2011-2020

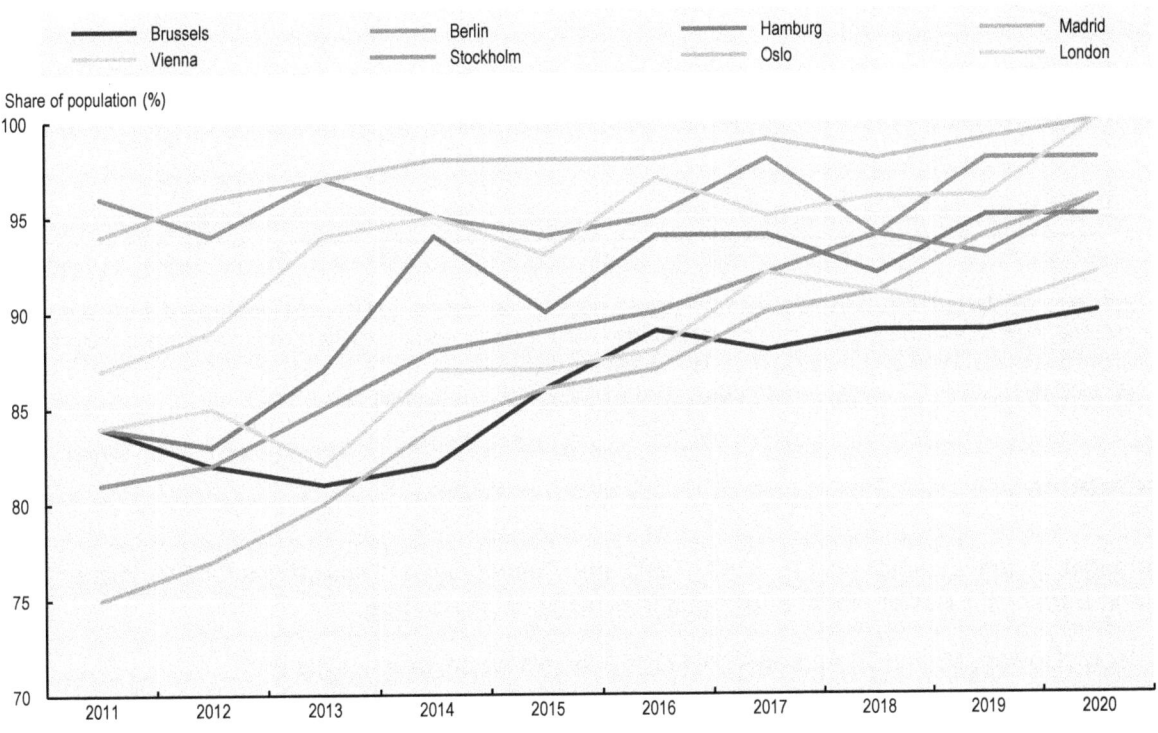

Source: Community survey on ICT usage by households and individuals, available on Eurostat [isoc_r_iuse_i].

While most people in Berlin use the internet regularly, almost half of Berlin's population does not perform basic tasks online. In comparison to other OECD metropolitan areas such as Oslo, London, Brussels or Hamburg, many more people in Berlin do not appear to use social networks, buy or sell goods online, or use online banking. While there could be several factors at play for those differences, the data might also suggest that many individuals in Berlin could lack the necessary familiarity and experience in pursuing tasks online. This, in turn, could indicate a lack of digital skills that goes beyond the minimal competency of simply using the internet for minimal tasks such as browsing or search queries. In a broader sense, such data appear to corroborate the widespread views expressed by employers in Berlin that many workers or job seekers do not meet the requirements in terms of digital skills that many jobs entail.

Figure 3.15. Only 45% of internet users in Berlin perform basic tasks online

Share of total internet users in Berlin performing basic tasks online, international comparison

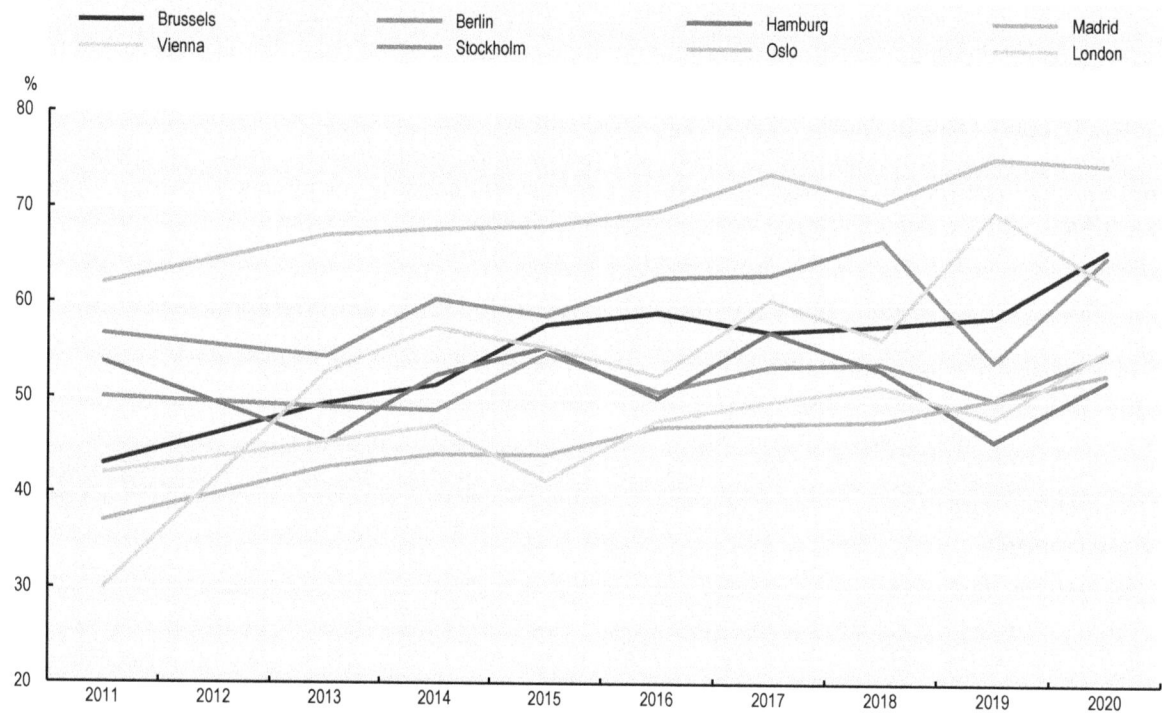

Note: Performing basic tasks online calculated as the unweighted average of those who replied they used social networks, sold or bought goods online and used online banking over the past three months. The denominator are those who used the internet over the past three months. Year 2012 imputed as average of year 2011 and 2013 due to lack of available data.
Source: Community survey on ICT usage by households and individuals, available on Eurostat [isoc_r_iuse_i].

References

Acemoglu, D. and D. Autor (2011), *Skills, Tasks and Technologies: Implications for Employment and Earnings*, Elsevier-North, https://economics.mit.edu/files/7006. [2]

Adalet McGowan, M. and D. Andrews (2017), "Skills mismatch, productivity and policies: Evidence from the second wave of PIAAC", *OECD Economics Department Working Papers*, No. 1403, OECD Publishing, Paris, https://dx.doi.org/10.1787/65dab7c6-en. [12]

Adalet McGowan, M. and D. Andrews (2015), "Labour Market Mismatch and Labour Productivity: Evidence from PIAAC Data", *OECD Economics Department Working Papers*, No. 1209, OECD Publishing, Paris, https://dx.doi.org/10.1787/5js1pzx1r2kb-en. [13]

Autor, D., F. Levy and R. Murnane (2003), "The Skill Content of Recent Technological Change: an", *The Quarterly Journal of Economics*, Vol. 118/3, pp. 1279-1333, https://economics.mit.edu/files/11574. [24]

Brinkman, J. (2015), "Big Cities and the Highly Educated: What's the Connection?", *Federal Reserve Bank of Philadelphia Research Department*. [21]

Brüning, N. and P. Mangeol (2020), "WHAT SKILLS DO EMPLOYERS SEEK IN GRADUATES? USING ONLINE JOB POSTING DATA TO SUPPORT POLICY AND PRACTICE IN HIGHER EDUCATION OECD Education Working Paper No. 231", http://www.oecd.org/termsandconditions. (accessed on 8 December 2021). [18]

Château, J., R. Dellink and E. Lanzi (2014), "An Overview of the OECD ENV-Linkages Model: Version 3", *OECD Environment Working Papers*, No. 65, OECD Publishing, Paris, https://dx.doi.org/10.1787/5jz2qck2b2vd-en. [11]

Coibion, O., Y. Gorodnichenko and M. Weber (2020), "Labor Markets During the COVID-19 Crisis: A Preliminary View", National Bureau of Economic Research, Cambridge, MA, http://dx.doi.org/10.3386/w27017. [20]

Crawford Urban, M. and S. Johal (2020), *Understanding the Future of Skills: Trends and Global Policy*, https://fsc-ccf.ca/wp-content/uploads/2020/01/UnderstandingTheFutureOfSkills-PPF-JAN2020-EN.pdf. [5]

Frey, C. and M. Osborne (2017), "The future of employment: How susceptible are jobs to computerisation?", *Technological Forecasting and Social Change*, Vol. 114, pp. 254-280, https://doi.org/10.1016/j.techfore.2016.08.019. [3]

Ludolph, L. (2021), *The Value of Formal Host-Country Education for the Labour Market Position of Refugees: Evidence from Austria*, http://www.RePEc.org. [23]

Nedelkoska, L. and G. Quintini (2018), "Automation, skills use and training", *OECD Social, Employment and Migration Working Papers*, No. 202, OECD Publishing, Paris, https://dx.doi.org/10.1787/2e2f4eea-en. [4]

OECD (2021), *Future-Proofing Adult Learning in London, United Kingdom*, OECD Reviews on Local Job Creation, OECD Publishing, Paris, https://dx.doi.org/10.1787/c546014a-en. [7]

OECD (2021), *OECD Regional Outlook 2021: Addressing COVID-19 and Moving to Net Zero Greenhouse Gas Emissions*, OECD Publishing, Paris, https://dx.doi.org/10.1787/17017efe-en. [10]

OECD (2021), *OECD Skills Outlook 2021: Learning for Life*, OECD Publishing, Paris, https://dx.doi.org/10.1787/0ae365b4-en. [22]

OECD (2020), *OECD Employment Outlook 2020: Worker Security and the COVID-19 Crisis*, OECD Publishing, Paris, https://dx.doi.org/10.1787/1686c758-en. [16]

OECD (2020), *Preparing for the Future of Work in Canada*, OECD Reviews on Local Job Creation, OECD Publishing, Paris, https://dx.doi.org/10.1787/05c1b185-en. [6]

OECD (2019), *Under Pressure: The Squeezed Middle Class*, OECD Publishing, Paris, https://dx.doi.org/10.1787/689afed1-en. [9]

OECD (2018), *Good Jobs for All in a Changing World of Work: The OECD Jobs Strategy*, OECD Publishing, Paris, https://dx.doi.org/10.1787/9789264308817-en. [1]

OECD (2018), *Job Creation and Local Economic Development 2018: Preparing for the Future of Work*, OECD Publishing, Paris, https://dx.doi.org/10.1787/9789264305342-en. [14]

OECD (2018), *OECD Employment Outlook 2018*, OECD Publishing, Paris, https://dx.doi.org/10.1787/empl_outlook-2018-en. [17]

OECD (2017), *OECD Employment Outlook 2017*, OECD Publishing, Paris, https://dx.doi.org/10.1787/empl_outlook-2017-en. [8]

OECD (2015), *In It Together: Why Less Inequality Benefits All*, OECD Publishing, Paris, https://dx.doi.org/10.1787/9789264235120-en. [15]

OECD (2010), *Higher Education in Regional and City Development - Berlin, Germany*, https://www.oecd.org/germany/45359278.pdf (accessed on 19 January 2022). [19]

Notes

[1] Technological change is a major reason for the disappearance of middle-skilled jobs. Information and Communication Technology (ICT) mainly offers a substitute for middle-skill jobs. Thus, technological developments and their capacity to replace routine tasks are drivers of job polarisation, as the impact of technology on jobs varies across the skills distribution. Across industries, occupations, and education levels, digitalisation is linked with reduced labour input of routine manual and routine cognitive tasks. Meanwhile, technological change and digitalisation are associated with an increase in non-routine cognitive tasks (Autor, Levy and Murnane, 2003[24]). As middle-skill jobs, such as clerical and production jobs, often entail routine tasks, they are easier to automate. In contrast, low-skill jobs often also involve non-routine manual tasks, which are more difficult to automate.

[2] See https://arbeitsmarktmonitor.arbeitsagentur.de/faktencheck/fachkraefte/karte/515/0/0/F7/ (accessed 01/02/2022).

[3] See https://statistik.arbeitsagentur.de/DE/Navigation/Statistiken/Interaktive-Angebote/Fachkraeftebedarf/Fachkraeftebedarf-Nav.html;jsessio-nid=E704DDDFFE03994804403BACEE25CA91 (accessed 01/02/2022).

[4] See https://statistik.arbeitsagentur.de/DE/Navigation/Statistiken/Interaktive-Angebote/Fachkraeftebedarf/Engpassanalyse-Nav.html;jsessionid=E704DDDFFE03994804403BACEE25CA91 (accessed 01/02/2022).

[5] See https://con.arbeitsagentur.de/prod/entgeltatlas/beruf/3641 (accessed 01/02/2022).

4 Strengthening adult learning for inclusion and social mobility

This chapter analyses the continuous education and training (CET) ecosystem in Berlin. It does so in three parts. The first part provides a descriptive overview of CET participation in Berlin and puts Berlin's CET participation rates into both a national and international perspective. The second part provides an overview of Berlin's CET landscape, focussing on the institutional setting and existing policy instruments to increase participation in continuous education and training. It further describes existing bottlenecks in service provision. Best-practice examples from other German federal states and OECD cities are provided throughout the chapter. The third part then zooms in on promising initiatives that could help Berlin increase CET participation among vulnerable population groups.

In Brief

CET participation in Berlin has not yet kept up with its rapidly changing labour market

- **CET participation in Berlin is low compared to other OECD cities and German federal states.** Participation in formal and non-formal CET outside the workplace is low in Berlin compared to international peer cities across the OECD. Labour Force Survey data shows that around 10% of individuals aged 25 to 64 participated in formal or non-formal education and training outside the workplace in the four weeks prior to their interview in 2019. Microsensus data shows that less than 14% of individuals aged 15 or over participated in formal or non-formal work-related CET in the year 2019, the lowest share among Germany's federal states.

- **One of the key reasons for the low CET participation rate in Berlin is the large share of microenterprises, self-employed and own-account workers.** In Berlin, 83% of Small and medium-sized enterprises (SMEs) employ fewer than five employees. In addition, 13.5% of Berlin's total employed were self-employed in 2019, a much higher share than in all other German federal states. The majority among the self-employed are own-account workers, i.e. self-employed without any employees. In Berlin, both awareness of existing measures as well as the take-up of instruments remains very low among Berlin's microenterprises, suggesting that support beyond financial incentives is necessary to increase CET participation among employees in SMEs. Own-account workers in Berlin currently receive little support to overcome their financial and time constraints to participate in life-long learning.

- **The wide range of adult learning guidance services in Berlin caters to many different groups specifically but can also make it difficult for learners to navigate through offers.** Next to the offers by the *Bundesagentur für Arbeit* ("Federal Employment Agency"; BA), different Senate departments offer CET guidance services to a range of target groups, with some overlap. Among the existing online offers, the visibility of the comprehensive *Berliner Weiterbildungsdatenbank* ("CET database Berlin"; WDB) could be improved and become a promising tool to facilitate participation in learning and training offers. Such efforts could form part of a wider public outreach campaign to foster awareness of the benefits of lifelong learning.

- **CET and career guidance measures exist for migrants, but offers are scattered and some synergies are left unexploited in Berlin.** The courses in highest demand in Berlin's *Volkshochschulen* ("Adult education centres"; VHS) are German language courses taken by migrants and refugees. However, Berlin's VHS currently do not offer institutionalised career, education or labour market guidance to these groups. Among the non-institutionalised existing measures, it is not always clear why some guidance services only target refugees, but leave out other migrants who likely face similar obstacles on the labour market.

- **Promising initiatives that target vulnerable groups have emerged within Berlin's social economy.** Berlin has an active social economy that supports and complements adult learning measures by the Public Employment Services (PES), the federal government, and the federal state government. For example, social economy actors target groups such as functionally illiterate adults through basic education and literacy courses as well as refugees through courses on digital skills that do not require German language skills.

CET participation in Berlin: a national and international comparison

Continuing learning beyond initial education is essential for adults to keep up with a rapidly changing world of work. Labour market megatrends in digitalization, the automation of production processes and a changing demography impact the skills required to perform jobs. Participation in CET measures that aim to update and upgrade skills continuously is therefore essential to maintain the employability of people and increase labour force participation. Adult learning systems therefore have to be evaluated on participation metrics and obstacles to participation in adult learning that could prevent some individuals or groups from participating in education and training beyond their initial education. This section provides an overview of formal and non-formal CET participation in Berlin and puts participation rates into national and international perspective.

There are three types of CET participation: formal, non-formal and informal education. Different survey data sources consider different types of learning when asking survey participants if they engaged in education and training in a specified period prior to the interview. The reference period also largely differs between data sources. Thus, any national and international comparison needs to ensure comparability by specifying both the type of learning or education it refers to and the reference period it considers. Definitions of the three different types of learning and how these are measured in the survey data used within this report are detailed in Box 4.1.

Box 4.1. Differences between formal, informal and non-formal education and their measurement in different German data sources

To measure and compare participation in training and education across countries and regions, it is necessary to define the type of education and training the individuals engage in. The reference period needs to be considered to make data sources comparable.

Types of training

Three different types of education are typically distinguished in official data sources (OECD, 2021[1]).

Formal education and training: Formal education is intentional learning within institutions recognised by government authorities, which last for a minimum of one semester. Examples of formal education include upper secondary school and university studies.

Non-formal education and training: Non-formal education is intentional, institutionalised learning of either less than one semester within institutions recognised by government authorities, or education and training outside educational institutions. Non-formal education includes courses, workshops, guided on-the-job training and seminars.

Informal education and training: Informal education refers to less organised forms of intentional learning outside an institutional environment. Informal education can happen in daily life, in a family environment or in the workplace.

Main data sources to measure participation in training

Three main data sources are used within this report to compare CET participation in Berlin to other regions and cities.

The first is the **European Labour Force Survey (EU-LFS)**. The EU-LFS reports data on formal and informal education individuals participated in within four weeks prior to the interview. Importantly, the EU-LFS does not include guided on-the-job training (GOTJ), one of the main forms of non-formal education and training in most EU member states (European Centre for the Development of Vocational

Training, 2015[2]). EU-LFS based CET participation rates are calculated as the number of 25 to 64 year olds who participated in training, divided by the total population aged 25 to 64.

The second data source used for this study is the **German Microcensus**. The German Microcensus captures job-related training and retraining measures such as lectures or weekend courses, the attendance of technician or master schools as well as the attendance of job-related courses and seminars. Work-related training can take place within the company or at the workplace, in special training centres of companies, associations or chambers of crafts. It can also take place as distance learning. A requirement for counting as a participant in GOTJ is a completed initial education or adequate work experience. Courses that serve the general education or formal vocational training do not count as work-related training. The report uses the measure as a crude proxy for GOTJ; the data captures both training at the workplace and away from it. The CET participation rates based on the Microcensus are calculated as the share of individuals in the labour force aged 15 and above who participated in GOTJ over the past 12 months, divided by the total labour force.

The two measures based on the EU-LFS and the Microcensus thus complement each other. However, the different reference periods, the different underlying populations as well as the limited overlap between the two mean that they cannot be added up to an aggregate measure. Both measures are estimates based on the sampled population rather than population counts.

A third data source referenced in this report is the **IAB Establishment Panel**. The IAB Establishment Panel is an annual survey of approximately 16 000 businesses, representative on the federal state level. Two CET measures can be calculated based on the survey: The first measure is the share of businesses offering education and training. Surveyed companies are classified as offering CET if they either offered training themselves during working hours or covered (parts of) the costs of internal or external training courses for at least one of their employees within the first two quarters of the given year. The denominator is then the total number of companies. The second measure is the share of employees that participated in job-related training in the first two quarters of the year. Surveyed businesses are asked to estimate (or, if possible, accurately count) the number of employees who participated in CET over the past six months. This number is then summed up over all companies within a given region and the sum is then divided by the total number of employees in the region.

Despite broadly capturing the same metric, the German Microcensus and the IAB Establishment Panel can show very different CET participation rates. The main reason is the underlying population: The Microcensus-based CET participation estimates are calculated as a share of the entire labour force, which includes both the unemployed and the employed aged 15 and above. The employed in the Microcensus also include own-account workers, a group excluded from the IAB Establishment Panel. For example, in Berlin, own-account workers made up 11% of all employed in 2017 (Senatsverwaltung für Integration, 2019[3]).

It should further be stressed that none of the three CET participation measures used within this study includes informal education or training. Unlike the German Microcensus and the EU-LFS, the IAB Establishment Panel does not explicitly exclude informal learning. However, it is unclear to what extent employers are able to factor in informal learning when estimating the number of CET participants within their company. The inclusion of informal education and training is also the main reason why CET participation rates in Germany calculated based on other (Eisermann, Janik and Kruppe, 2014[4]).

Source: European Centre for the Development of Vocational Training (2015[2]), *Job-related adult learning and continuing vocational training in Europe a statistical picture*; Senatsverwaltung für Integration (2019[3]), *Solo-Selbstständige arbeiten oft prekär und schlecht bezahlt*; Eisermann, Janik and Kruppe (2014[4]), *Participation in adult education: The reasons for inconsistent participation rates in different sources of data*.

CET participation does not capture all human capital accumulation, especially in cities. As a result, baseline statistics on formal an informal CET participation rates are likely to underestimate the full extent of learning and training that raise human capital. Of the types of learning described in Box 4.1, informal learning is not included in the data analysis conducted for this study. Academic research on learning in big cities shows that the relatively higher amount of social and business contacts in cities facilitate informal learning. Box 4.2 describes the link between population density and informal learning. Consequently, data on CET participation in Berlin comes with the caveat that it might only offer an incomplete picture. To mitigate this issue, this section also compares Berlin to other major OECD metropolitan areas that would have similar patterns of informal learning.

Box 4.2. The link between population density and informal learning

A study by de la Roca and Puga (2017[5]) finds that higher wages in cities are not explained by the spatial sorting of more productive workers into big cities, nor by static agglomeration advantages of big cities. Instead, workers who move to cities receive an immediate static premium and gain valuable work experience quickly upon arrival. Further evidence suggests that these findings can be generalised to an even larger degree: The size of the labour market where the work experience was acquired partly explains differences in future wages (Peters, 2020[6]).

The main takeaway of these studies is that learning in big cities – or dense urban environments – often takes place outside of classrooms.

Source: de la Roca and Puga (2017[5]), *Learning by Working in Big Cities;* Peters (2020[6]), *Dynamic agglomeration economies and learning by working in specialised regions.*

Participation in formal and non-formal CET outside the workplace is low in Berlin compared to international peers across the OECD. Figure 4.1 shows the share of individuals aged 25 to 64 who participated in formal or non-formal (excluding on-the-job) education and training in the four weeks prior to the interview between 2010 and 2020. The graph compares Berlin to other OECD cities. Berlin's CET participation rate remained constant at around 10% over the observation period. Internationally, Brussels (Belgium) and Warsaw (Poland) show similar participation rates in formal and non-formal (excluding on-the-job) education and training. Other OECD cities such as Helsinki (Finland), Stockholm (Sweden) or Zurich (Switzerland) have much higher participation rates than Berlin. In 2020, participation rates stood at 30.8%, 30.1% and 32.9% respectively in these cities. In London (United Kingdom) and Paris (France), the capital regions of similarly sized European countries, the most recent reported participation rates were 16% and 13% respectively, well-above the level of Berlin.

In Germany, CET participation rates in formal and non-formal education in Berlin are on a par with other city states and higher than in non-city federal states. Figure 4.2 shows the share of individuals aged 25 to 64 who participated in formal or non-formal (excluding guided on-the-job) education and training in the four weeks prior to the interview between 2010 and 2020. The graph compares Berlin to the other German federal states. The national comparison shows that Berlin's participation rate in formal or non-formal (excluding on-the-job) education and training is on the same level as Hamburg's and Bremen's, the other German city states. In 2020, participation rates in these cities were 10.0% and 9.4% respectively. All non-city German federal states report slightly lower participation, down to 5.3% in the federal state of Saarland in 2020. Between 2019 and 2020, participation increased only in Berlin and the federal states of Nordrhein-Westfalen. It should be noted that these participation rates are unadjusted and do not account for differences in age and education of the respective population in the different federal states.

Figure 4.1. Participation in education and training that excludes guided on-the-job training is low in Berlin compared to other OECD metropolitan areas

Share of individuals aged 25-64 who participated in lifelong learning within the four weeks prior to the interview

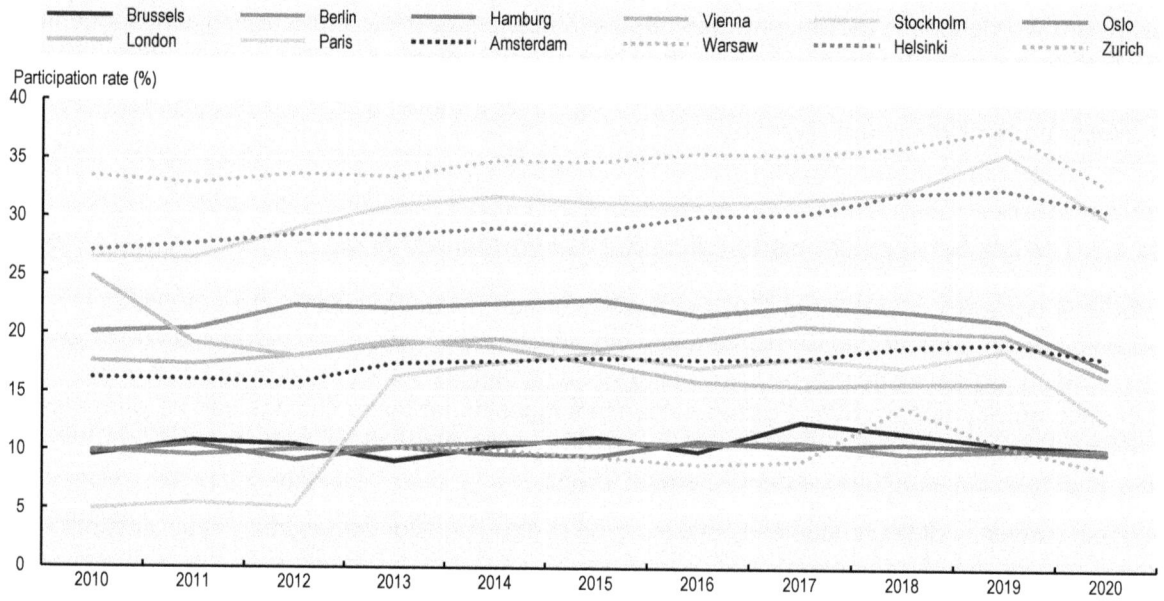

Note: Brussels refers to the Brussels capital region. Paris refers to the Île de France region. Amsterdam refers to the Noord-Nederland region. The data does not include guided on-the-job training.
Source: Eurostat Regional Database [trng_lfse_04], based on EU-LFS data.

Figure 4.2. Participation in education and training that excludes guided on-the-job training is high in Berlin compared to other German federal states

Share of individuals aged 25-64 who participated in lifelong learning within the four weeks prior to the interview

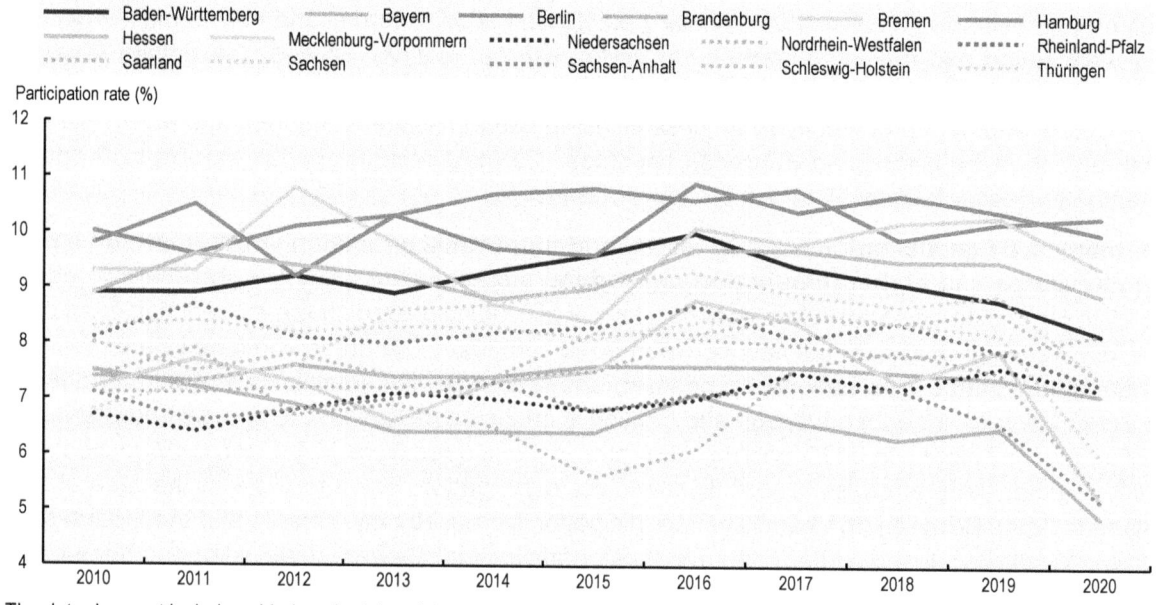

Note: The data does not include guided on-the-job training.
Source: Eurostat Regional Database [trng_lfse_04], based on EU-LFS data.

Berlin lags behind all other German federal states for work-related CET. While Berlin has relatively high CET participation outside the workplace the picture is much less favourable for work-related formal and non-formal CET. Based on the most recent Microsensus data, less than 14% of individuals aged 15 or above participated in formal or non-formal work-related CET in 2019. In Sachsen and Thüringen, the two states with the highest participation, around 21% and 20% of the labour force participated in such CET offers respectively (Figure 4.3).

Figure 4.3. Berlin lags behind other German federal states for work-related formal and non-formal CET participation

Share of individuals in the labour force aged 15 and above with completed initial education who participated in formal or non-formal work-related CET over the past 12 months, 2019

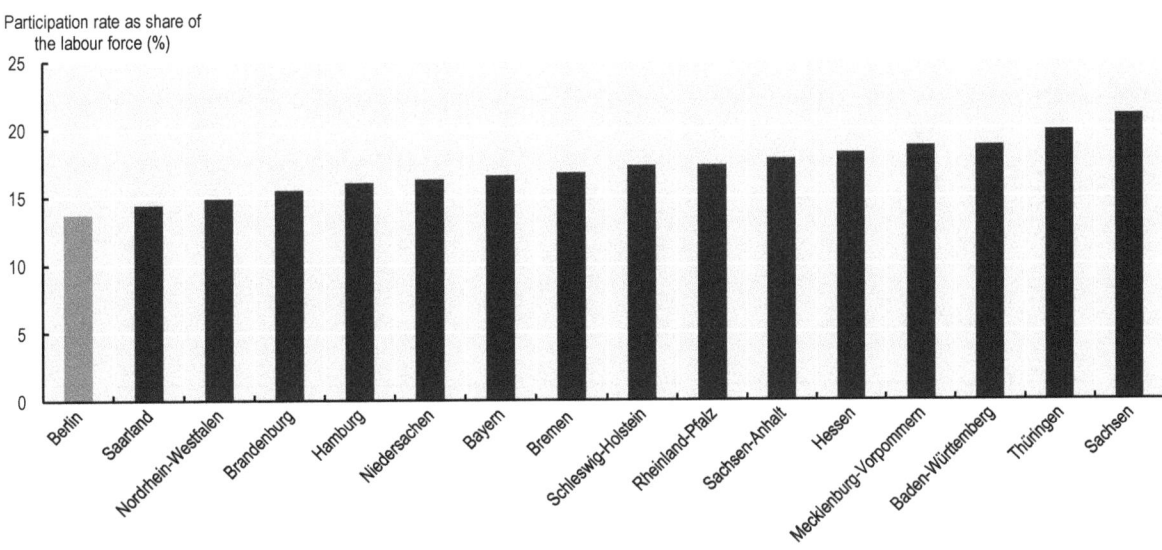

Note: Work-related CET participation refers to any participation in further education and training as well as retraining programmes of individuals aged 15 and above, either on the job or outside the job. Participation in CET requires completed initial education. General adult education for purposes other than professional development is not included in the CET measure. The denominator is the regional labour force ("Erwerbspersonen").
Source: OECD calculations based on Microcensus Germany.

Low work-related CET participation rates in Berlin are not a new phenomenon. For the period since 2014 for which comparable statistics based on the German Microcensus can be produced, work-related CET participation was constant at around 14% of the labour force (Figure 4.4, Panel B). The estimated total number of participants grew from 253 000 in 2014 to 272 000 in 2019, in line with the growth of the labour force in Berlin (Panel A). Consequently, work-related CET has not increased in Berlin despite its growing importance in a rapidly changing labour market (see Chapter 2). The data from 2019 do not take account the effects of the pandemic. Since COVID-19 caused a range of social-distancing measures and took a financial toll on many firms, it likely reduced work-related CET further.

Unique demographic, social and economic characteristics by themselves cannot explain the low CET participation rate in Berlin. A 2018 study by the *Deutsche Institut für Erwachsenenbildung* ("German Institute for Adult Education"; DIE) calculates expected CET participation rates in all German federal states accounting for structural regional differences, such as the local age structure, average education levels and differences in average income. Holding these variables constant, the study shows that Berlin only utilised 77.4% of its CET potential in 2015, the second lowest value in Germany. Only the federal state of Saarland utilised less of its CET potential (75.4%). On the other hand, some federal states such as Baden-Württemberg and Rheinland-Pfalz managed to reach CET participation rates above their potential, with 119.7% and 117.3% respectively (DIE and Bertelsmann Stiftung, 2018[7]).

Figure 4.4. The share of Berlin's population participating in work-related formal and non-formal CET has remained constant over time

Total number of individuals (Panel A) and share of individuals (Panel B) in the labour force aged 15 and above with completed initial education who participated in formal or non-formal work-related CET over the past 12 months, 2014 to 2019

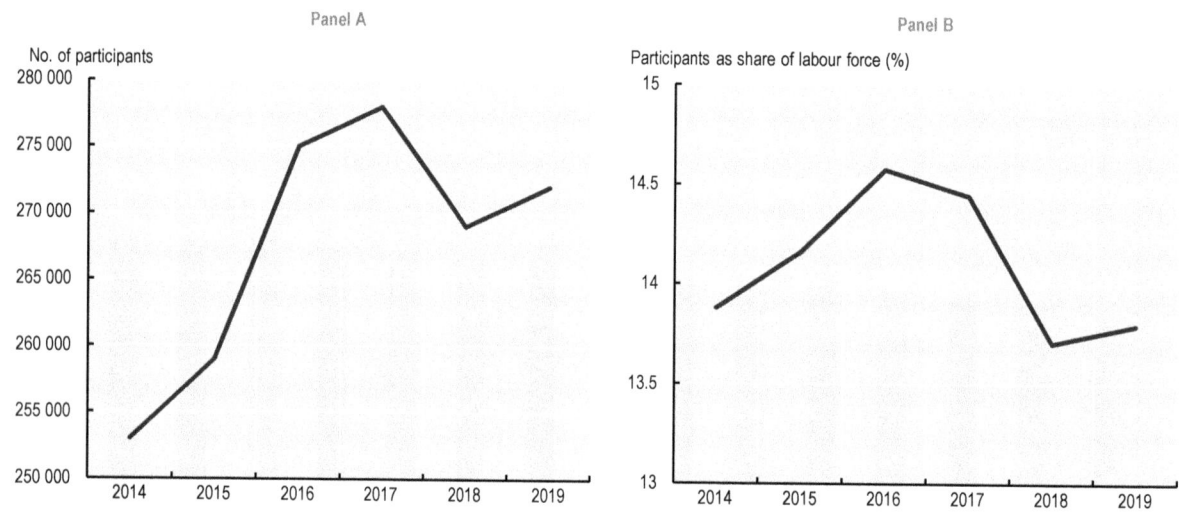

Note: Work-related CET participation refers to any participation in further education and training as well as retraining programmes of individuals aged 15 and above, either on the job or outside the job. Participation in CET requires completed initial education. General adult education for purposes other than professional development is not included in the CET measure. The denominator of the right-hand side figure is the regional labour force ("Erwerbspersonen").
Source: OECD elaboration on Microcensus Germany.

Local demographic, social and economic characteristics can only account for one third of the differences in CET participation rates across Germany. Thus, other factors such as the quality of CET, visibility of the different CET offers, cooperation between different local CET actors and the CET guidance infrastructure are likely to play an important role (DIE and Bertelsmann Stiftung, 2018[7]).

CET offered by Berlin's companies is heavily dependent on the company size. Table 4.1 shows the share of companies offering education and training courses to employees by company size. The first column shows the size of the company measured by the number of employees. The second column shows the share of companies in the respective size category that offered education and training courses to their employees in 2019, the year before the COVID-19 outbreak. In 2019, only 49% of companies with fewer than 10 employees offered education and training opportunities to their employees. This share rises sharply with the size of the company: Among companies that employed 10 to 49 employees in 2019, the share stood at 70%, while almost all larger companies employing 50 or more individuals offered employees some form of job-related training.

The share of companies offering training and education courses dropped sharply during the COVID-19 pandemic, especially among very small enterprises. Comparing the second and third column of Table 4.1 reveals that the share of companies offering training and education to employees dropped sharply in Berlin. In 2019, 57% of all Berlin based companies offered some form of education or training to employees. In 2020, that share dropped to 33%. While companies of all sizes reduced their CET offer, very small enterprises (less than 10 employees) recorded the largest relative fall (-42%), followed by enterprises with 10 to 49 employees (-40%).

Table 4.1. CET offered by companies of all sizes dropped sharply during COVID-19

Education and training offered by company size in Berlin, 2019 and 2020

Size of the company by number of employees	Share of companies offering CET in 2019	Share of companies offering CET in 2020
<10	49%	28%
10 to 49	70%	42%
50 to 249	91%	65%
250+	97%	76%
Total	57%	33%

Source: IAB Establishment Panel, waves 2019 and 2020.

The type of training offered by companies in Berlin also depends on the company size. Data from an *Industrie- und Handelskammer Berlin* ("Chamber of Commerce and Industry"; IHK Berlin) survey conducted in 2019 shows that smaller companies more often rely almost exclusively on self-studying instruments to train their employees. Figure 4.5 shows that 53% and 60% of Berlin's companies (that are IHK Berlin members) offer self-studying using digital media and self-studying using non-digital media respectively, with little variation across companies of different size. However, companies with larger numbers of employees more often offer non-self-studying training instruments. For example, only 37% of companies that employ fewer than 10 employees offer in-service seminars, compared to 94% of companies employing between 200 and 499 salaried employees. Similar trends can be seen in coaching and mentoring, management training and the possibility of pursuing formal studies alongside employment. The gap between the share of the smallest companies and the share of companies employing between 200 and 499 employees that offered these types of training in 2019 stood at 26 percentage points, 32 percentage points and 36 percentage points respectively.

SMEs and microenterprises in particular tend to underinvest into CET due to a lack of resources and insufficient investment incentives. The issue of little CET investment in small companies is not a Berlin-specific problem and exists for two main reasons: First, SMEs may lack the financial and human resources to offer job-related training. Second, they may lack the incentives to invest into their staff since more qualified staff may demand higher wages; if SMEs are unwilling to pay workers according to their additional (marginal) productivity after new skills are acquired, these workers may leave the firm and small businesses suffer a net loss from the training investment (Brunello et al., 2020[8]).

However, the lack of awareness of training needs, the lack of capacity to assess skill needs and the lack of knowledge about existing training opportunities may also play a role for underinvestment into CET in SMEs. Recent OECD research shows that very small SMEs in particular often do not have their own human resource department and rarely employ specialists on skill development. Assessing skill needs, developing targeted training measures and obtaining external funding are often time-intensive tasks that require specialist employees (OECD, 2021[9]).

Investment into CET by small companies in Berlin may therefore be too low. Additional investment into CET leads to upskilling in workers that allows them to transition into higher quality jobs, earn higher salaries and create additional tax income. Incentivising SMEs to invest more into CET through financial and logistic support can thus be desirable if there is evidence that such measures could lead to an increase in structured education and training offered within or by the small company.

Figure 4.5. Small companies in Berlin rely heavily on self-studying methods

Type of CET offered by size of the enterprise in Berlin, 2019

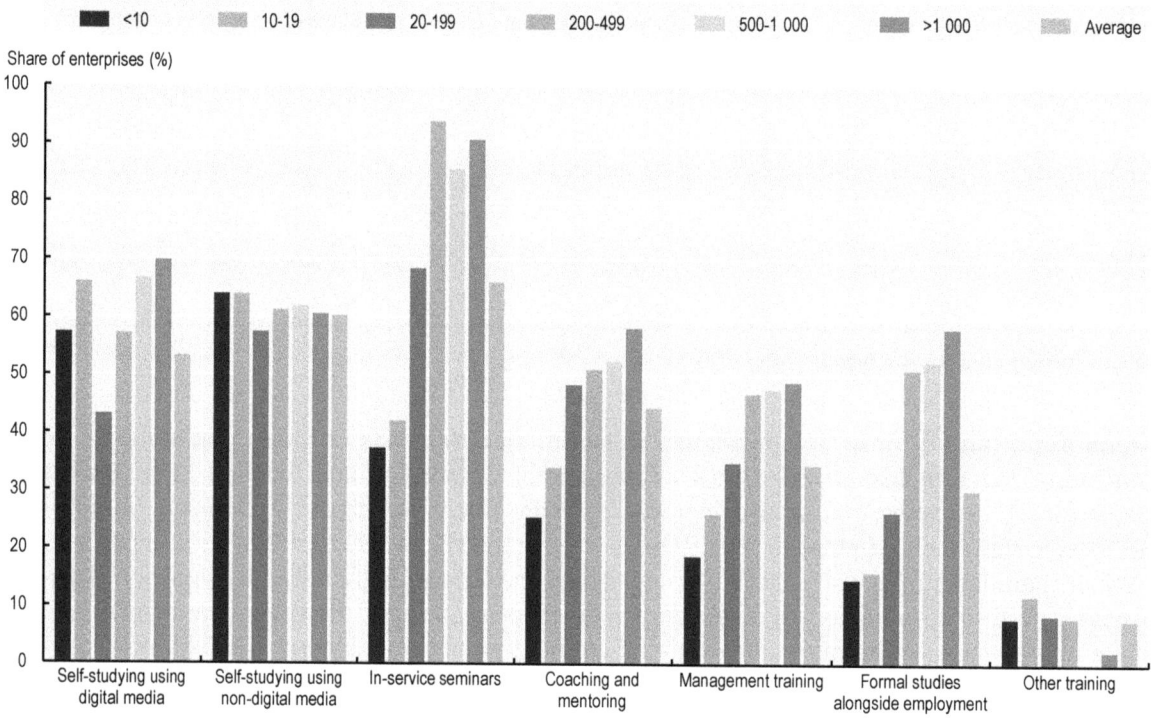

Note: "Management training" refers to the German *Aufstiegsfortbildung*, a type of training that aims to qualify employees to take on management responsibilities and advance their careers.
Source: Chamber of Commerce and Industry of Berlin (IHK Berlin), "Aus- und Weiterbildungsumfrage 2019".

The share of very small businesses among SMEs in Berlin is slightly higher than in other German regions, exacerbating the problem of underinvestment into CET. In Berlin, 83% of SMEs employ fewer than five employees, compared to 81% in Germany. In total, 58% of Berlin's working population was employed by SMEs in 2018 (KfW Research, 2018[10]). Even small differences in company size among SMEs may make a large difference in CET offers. Table 4.2 and Figure 4.5 show that training offers drop sharply in microenterprises, compared to SMEs with 20 or more employees.

Another factor that might hold back CET participation in Berlin is self-employment. The share of self-employed among all employed is much higher in Berlin than in other German federal states. Figure 2.11 shows that 13.5% of Berlin's total employed were self-employed in 2019, a share much larger than in all other German federal states. In addition to the large number of self-employed in Berlin, own-account workers made up 11% of all employed, corresponding to 74% of all self-employed (Senatsverwaltung für Integration, 2019[3]). In Germany as a whole, 54.4% of all self-employed were own-account workers in 2019. Thus, a much larger share of the self-employed in Berlin are own-account workers than in other German cities and regions.

Own-account workers tend to participate very little in continuous education and training, even compared to other self-employed. Across the OECD, CET participation among own-account workers is very low compared to all other workers. OECD analyses show that conditional on age, gender and education, only adults outside the labour force and the unemployed are less likely to participate in CET courses. Compared to the employed, own-account workers are 11% less likely to receive education or training. On the other hand, their willingness to participate in CET is similar to that of full-time employees (OECD, 2019[11]).

The low participation of own-account workers in education and training is explained in parts by their relatively stricter financial and time constraints. Own-account workers often work longer hours due to additional time needed to look for future work assignments. The cost of training is another major barrier to CET participation among own-account workers. Public financial support programmes typically target the employed or the unemployed, such that both the direct and the indirect costs of CET have to be borne by own-account workers themselves. Own-account workers also tend to have fewer legal rights to training since they lack union representation (OECD, 2019[11]).

In summary, Berlin's low CET participation in international comparison and its very low work-related CET in national comparison are likely caused by a combination of factors. The main challenge is the large share of very small firms, self-employed and own-account workers. The obstacles these groups face to participate in education and training in larger numbers were likely aggravated by the COVID-19 pandemic, which led to additional financial pressure and new challenges such as social distancing requirements within companies. Pre-existing trends towards the automation of production processes and the need for digital skills accelerated. Policies are therefore needed to re-invigorate CET in Berlin. The next section takes a closer look at Berlin's CET landscape.

Berlin's CET landscape: Funding and service delivery

As CET ultimately benefits the learner, there are important questions on when and how to use public funds to increase CET participation. CET is important as it prepares adults for their future careers and ensures that companies remain competitive by developing skills in their workforce that respond to changes in production processes. Thus, the main incentive to invest into CET lies with individuals and companies. Nevertheless, some individuals and companies face barriers to CET participation that well-targeted policy instruments can overcome. This section provides an overview of Berlin's CET landscape. It introduces the main actors in Berlin, distinguishes between different types of instruments used and analyses complementarities between services offered by the German federal government and the government of Berlin.

CET measures in Germany mostly receive funding from individuals and companies. Figure 4.6 shows funding of adult learning beyond initial education in Germany by different sources. In 2015 – the latest year for which a detailed funding breakdown is available – private individuals and companies were responsible for 38% and 43% of total funding respectively. Public funding accounted for the remaining 19%. The public funding comes from the BA and directly from the federal, regional and local governments in approximately equal parts. The BA is funded primarily through unemployment insurance contributions.

The CET landscape in Germany is characterised by a high degree of decentralisation. Individuals and enterprises are generally the main entities responsible for CET uptake and the provision of training. Within its governance structure, companies, the social and economic partners, CET providers and the government at national and federal state level are all involved in shaping CET offers and curricula (OECD, 2021[1]). On the one hand, such a decentralised system is widely recognised for achieving training provision that can be tailored to regional context. On the other hand, the coordination between different stakeholders that is required to make such a system efficient is a major challenge.

Figure 4.6. CET measures in Germany are mostly funded by individuals and companies

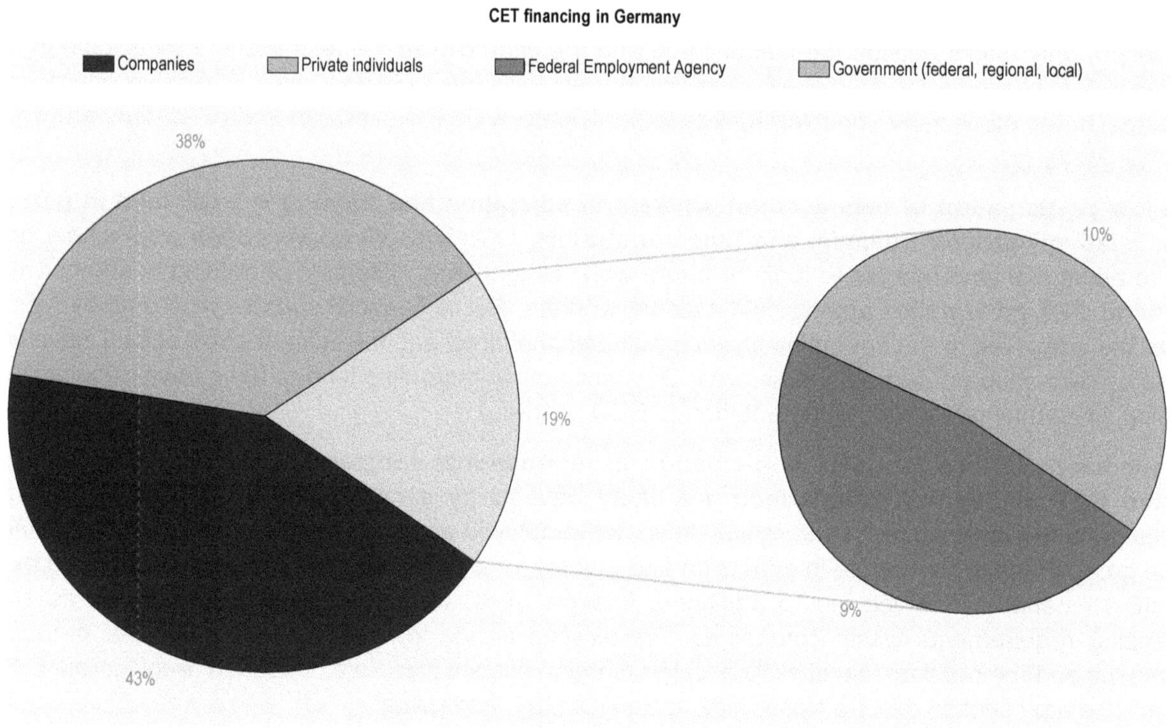

CET financing in Germany

- Companies
- Private individuals
- Federal Employment Agency
- Government (federal, regional, local)

Companies: 43%
Private individuals: 38%
Federal Employment Agency: 9%
Government (federal, regional, local): 10%
(19%)

Note: 2015 is latest data available. The Federal Employment Agency is funded primarily through unemployment insurance contributions.
Source: Dohmen and Cordes (2019[12])

The main actors in continuous education and training in Berlin

Fundamentally, three different types of CET in Berlin can be distinguished by their respective target group. The first type is CET offered to the unemployed in the form of active labour market policies (ALMPs). The primary goal of these measures is to integrate the unemployed back into the labour market, thus ensuring that skills match those demanded on the labour market and unemployment spells do not become too long. The second type is CET offered to the employed to build on their existing skills. The primary objective of such CET is to improve the labour market position of participants and ensure their adaptation to changing job skill requirements. The third type is general adult education, which offers a broad set of education and training courses. It is open to anyone in the population, regardless of age or employment status. Its objective is not primarily labour market related.

Different actors within the Berlin CET landscape are responsible for delivering CET guidance and education and training depending on the target group. Similar to other German federal states, a range of actors are involved in the guidance and delivery of CET:

- **The *Bundesagentur für Arbeit – Regionaldirektion Berlin-Brandenburg* ("Regional Directorate of the Federal Employment Agency – Berlin-Brandenburg"; BA)**; The BA is the German Public Employment Service (PES) and primarily focusses on the implementation of active labour market policies targeting the unemployed. Main services include linking clients to jobs and vocational training, career counselling, employer counselling, supporting job-related education and training as well as supporting the labour market integration of people with disability. Recently, the BA has also adopted measures geared towards CET of the employed. The BA has 10 regional directorates, with the directorate for Berlin-Brandenburg responsible for Berlin.

- The *Senatsverwaltung für Integration, Arbeit und Soziales* ("Berlin Senate Department for Integration, Labour and Social Affairs"; SenIAS); The SenIAS complements some measures offered by the BA through additional active labour market policies that target specific segments of both the employed and the unemployed.
- The *Job Centers*, jointly managed by the BA and the SenIAS, provide job market guidance and training to unemployed who are social assistance ("Hartz 4") recipients.
- The *Volkshochschulen* ("Adult Education Centres"; VHS), coordinated by the *Senatsverwaltung für Bildung, Jugend und Familie* ("Senate Department for Education, Youth and Family"; SenBJF); VHS offer general adult education open to anyone with courses generally not designed to support labour market prospects of participants.
- The *Landeszentrale für politische Bildung Berlin* ("Berlin's Agency for Civic Education"; LPBB); LPBB is a non-partisan institution to offer civic education under the supervision of SenBJF.
- The *Senatsverwaltung für Gesundheit, Pflege und Gleichstellung* ("Senate Department for Health, Care and Equality"; SenGPG); SenGPG offers job-related CET guidance to women specifically.
- **Private sector companies**; Private sector companies provide on-the-job training to employees at their own discretion.
- **Social partners;** Social partners such as trade unions and employer organisations and economic partners such as Chambers of Commerce and Trade and Chambers of Skilled Crafts play a key role in consulting on legislative processes at the federal state level, shaping regulations on ALMPs and formal vocational CET, negotiating collective and company agreements that affect CET provision (OECD, 2021[1]).
- **Non-governmental organisations (NGOs) and other social economy actors**; NGOs and other social economy actors target specific vulnerable segments of the population and provide training and education services that foster societal and labour market integration.

On the ground, job-related CET and CET counselling financed by the BA, the Job Centers and the SenIAS is primarily delivered through certified private *Bildungsträger* ("CET providers"). A certification as a CET provider can be obtained through a *fachkundige Stelle* ("expert office") listed in Germany's national accreditation body's database. A certification is required for all measures funded by the BA, the Job Centers and the SenIAS and is generally valid for three years. Employers offering on-the-job training generally do no need to be certified.

A striking feature of Berlin's CET landscape is the strict institutionalised distinction between job-related CET and general adult education. Work-related CET in Berlin is the joint responsibility of the BA Berlin-Brandenburg and SenIAS and delivered through certified CET providers. General adult learning is separated from these labour market related efforts. It is primarily delivered through the 12 VHS, which are institutions of the Berlin boroughs and are run and equipped by them at their own responsibility following the Berlin Schools Act (Section 123). The SenBJF performs regulatory tasks of citywide importance. This includes the regular publication of a comparative performance and quality development report and issuing of fee and remuneration regulations that are valid throughout Berlin's VHS. The independence of the VHS mean that they have almost complete discretion over their curricula.

The recent passing of a new law on adult learning in Berlin has further cemented the VHS as an integral part of Berlin's CET system. The law came into force in August 2021. It makes three major contributions to general adult education in Berlin: First, it provides legal safeguarding to the VHS and Berlin's LPBB. Second, adult learning providers can apply for official recognition as adult learning providers and use their status to apply for government funding. Third, the visibility of adult learning will be increased through regular reports on adult education in Berlin and the establishment of an *Erwachsenenbildungsbeirat* ("Adult Learning Advisory Board"). The new law is described in more detail in Box 4.3.

While positive for general adult education, the law exemplifies the strong divide between general adult education and labour market specific training in Berlin. For example, as shown in Box 4.3, the advisory board includes only one member jointly appointed by the *Industrie- und Handelskammer* ("Chamber of Commerce and Industry"), the *Berliner Handwerkskammer* ("Chamber of Crafts Berlin") or the *Vereinigung der Unternehmensverbände in Berlin und Brandenburg* ("Association of businesses in Berlin and Brandenburg"). Its membership is otherwise heavily skewed towards the representation of vulnerable minority groups. The link to Berlin's labour market and wider local economy is almost entirely missing. Other OECD cities such as London do not distinguish between civic education and work-related education and training as strictly, but rather acknowledge that economic and societal objectives are intertwined. Box 4.4 describes London's approach to adult learning in more detail.

Box 4.3. The new law on "adult learning in Berlin"

The new law on adult learning in Berlin was developed under the leadership of the SenBJF. It was passed in May 2021 and came into effect in August 2021. The law makes three major contributions to strengthening general adult education in Berlin.

First, the existing public adult education facilities in Berlin, the twelve local adult education centres (VHS) in Berlin and the Berlin Agency for Civic Education will be legally safeguarded. For the VHS, this means that important stipulations on course offers, equipment, digital infrastructure, quality standards for course instructors and participants are now legally enshrined. The Berlin Agency for Civic Education has a legal basis for the first time. Stable funding for education and training counselling is also part of the new law.

Second, any institution in Berlin that offers adult education can now apply for the status of a "recognized institution for adult education in Berlin". Such status then allows institutions and organisations to apply for newly created funding opportunities for important and innovative projects and programs. Funding is administered by the SenBJF.

Third, the law aims to improve public visibility of adult education through sparking public debate and advertisement of existing offers. An **adult education advisory board** will be set up for this purpose and a regular report on the status of adult education in Berlin will be published.

The new adult education advisory board brings together experts on adult education from different political, social, academic and business organisations, associations and institutions. Among its 31 board members, most are appointed due to their roles within the VHS system or are appointed directly and indirectly due to their political and administrative roles within Berlin's adult learning landscape. A large number of seats on the board is also reserved for representatives of minority groups. For example, one member each is appointed by the State Advisory Council for Integration and Migration Issues, the State Advisory Council for People with Disabilities, the Women's Political Advisory Council and an organization representing the interests of lesbians, gays, bisexuals and transgender and intersex people. On the other hand, the advisory board includes only one member jointly appointed by the Chamber of Commerce and Industry, the Chamber of Crafts Berlin and the Association of Businesses in Berlin and Brandenburg. The *Deutscher Gewerkschaftsbund* ("German Federation of Trade Unions") also appoints only one board member under the current configuration.

Source: Senatsverwaltung für Bildung (2021[13]), *Erwachsenenbildungsgesetz vom Parlament beschlossen: Historischer Tag für Lebenslanges Lernen in Berlin*; EBiG, § 16 - § 18 Teil 6 - Berliner Erwachsenenbildungsbeirat („Berlin adult education advisory board")

> **Box 4.4. Combining economic and societal objectives in adult learning in London, UK**
>
> Since 2019, the Greater London Authority (GLA) has been responsible for London's annual £320m Adult Education Budget (AEB) and has since produced several skills strategies that aim to upskill and reskill London's adult population. The *Skills Roadmap for London* is the latest skills strategy introduced by the Mayor of London in 2022. It has the main objective to "create a positive impact for Londoners in terms of both economic and social outcomes, including health and wellbeing" (Greater London Authority, 2022, p. 13[14]). The strategy will therefore be evaluated on key economic indicators such as improvements in London's employment rates and income levels, but also on wellbeing measures that relate to Londoners' life satisfaction. New survey data will be collected in London for this purpose.
>
> While the key objective of London's skills strategy is to support low-income individuals and households in moving into better jobs, the "no wrong door" approach lies at its centre: So-called *Integration Hubs* will ensure that different types of services collaborate and learning opportunities are provided independently of where individuals make first contact. These services include London's PES and the UK's *National Career Service* but also link support agencies working in health or services targeting disabled people and youth to adult learning opportunities.
>
> The skills strategy in London encompasses both general adult education and adult learning focussed on better labour market integration. Adult learning services provided through the AEB cover a wide range of work-related training but also offer training in basic literacy, numeracy, digital and core employability skills. English language courses target London's large migrant community.
>
> Source: Greater London Authority (2022[14]), *Skills Roadmap for London*.

Different types of continuous education and training instruments are delivered by the national and the federal state government of Berlin

Four policy instruments to encourage CET participation can be distinguished: CET guidance, financial incentives for individuals, education and training leave and financial incentives for companies. The general idea of all measures is to increase CET participation of individuals for whom the (long-term) benefits of education and training is larger than the direct or indirect (short-term) cost. Depending on the barrier to participation individuals face, different instruments can be deployed. CET guidance is used to raise awareness of CET services and increase participation of individuals who either did not know about existing offers or were not able to navigate these offers on their own. Education and training leave improves the conditions for CET participation by removing work-related time constraints that hamper participation rates. Financial incentives loosen financial constraints of individuals or companies or incentivise participation of individuals who may be unaware of the benefits.

Guidance on education and training

A plethora of CET guidance providers exist in Berlin. Table 4.2 gives an overview of the different CET guidance offered in Berlin, listed by the actors involved and their respective target groups. The main guidance providers are the SenIAS in its *Berliner Beratung zu Bildung und Beruf* ("Berlin Guidance on Education and Profession network"; BBB) and the BA's *Lebensbegleitende Berufsberatung im Erwerbsleben* ("Lifelong Vocational Guidance for adults in employment"; LBBiE). Smaller-scale guidance offers exist, with some complementing existing services offered by the main providers (*IQ-Netzwerk, Grundbildungszentrum Berlin*) and some existing for historical reasons (*Berufsperspektiven für Frauen*). CET guidance offers in the Berlin's VHS also exist, but are currently limited in scope, an observation discussed in more detail in section 3.2. The BA and the Job Centers also provide CET guidance to the unemployed specifically.

The CET guidance offered by the BA is open to all individuals, while SenIAS also targets some population groups specifically. The SenIAS operates a network of counselling centres. The network consists of seven career guidance centres that are open to all individuals and three more specialised centres. The specialised centres target individuals seeking further formal education (*Fachberatung berufliche Qualifizierung*), SMEs (*Qualifizierungsberatung in KMU*), migrants seeking language training (*Erfolg mit Sprache und Abschluss*) and refugees seeking general career guidance (*Mobile Beratung zu Bildung und Beruf für geflüchtete Menschen*; MoBiBe). Geographically, the counselling centres are spread out evenly across Berlin's boroughs (OECD, 2022[15]).

Table 4.2. CET guidance in Berlin

Overview of CET guidance offered in Berlin by provider and target group

Original name	English name	Actors involved (incl. funders)	Target group
Berliner Beratung zu Bildung und Beruf, BBB	Berlin Guidance on Education and Profession network	Senate Department for Integration, Labour and Social Affairs, SenIAS	All individuals
Fachberatung berufliche Qualifizierung, FbQu	Vocational qualification counselling	SANQ e. V.	Individuals seeking a formal diploma via partial qualifications
Erfolg mit Sprache und Abschluss, EMSA	Success with language and qualification	Arbeit und Bildung e. V.	Migrants
Qualifizierungsberatung in KMU	Qualification guidance for SMEs	GesBiT mbH	SMEs
Mobile Beratung zu Bildung und Beruf für geflüchtete Menschen, MoBiBe	Mobile counselling on education and careers for refugees	KOBRA (Berliner Frauenbund 1945 e.V.), Senate Department for Health, Care and Equality	Refugees
Lebensbegleitende Berufsberatung im Erwerbsleben, LBBiE	Lifelong Vocational Guidance for adults in employment	BA	All individuals
Volkshochschulen, VHS	Network of adult education centres	VHS	All individuals
IQ-Netzwerk	IQ-Network	BMAS, ESF, BAMF, BMBF, BA	Migrants
Berufsperspektiven für Frauen	Guidance network Career Progression for Women	Senate Department for Health, Care and Equality	Women
Grund-Bildungs-Zentrum Berlin, GBZ	Centre for Basic Education	Senate Department for Integration, Labour and Social Affairs, VHS	Low-qualified adults

Source: OECD (2022[15]).

All centres offer a wide range of CET guidance services, with some overlap between the services provided by the SenIAS and the BA. These services include counselling on formal education and training, professional (re-)orientation, CV writing, access to employment, career development, application procedures, CET while employed, learning strategies and sources of CET funding. Additional in-house services include the mapping of skills and formal education, the provision of a computer to facilitate the browsing of online databases, and support with the administrative steps in applications for jobs and education measures (OECD, 2022[15]). While both the SenIAS and the BA offer comprehensive CET guidance services, navigating through different very similar offers may not always be straightforward and could potentially discourage some individuals.

An overview of adult learning and CET offers is available online through national databases such as *Kursnet* ("Course net"). Kursnet is the BA's main nationwide online platform that functions as a search tool for CET offers. Other nationwide online tools hosted by the BA include *Karriere und Weiterbildung* ("Career and CET"), *Erkundungstool Check-U* ("Exploratory Tool Check-U"), *Berufsentwicklungsnavigator* ("Career Development Navigator"), *berufe.tv* ("jobs.tv"), *berufsfeld-info.de* ("Occupational Field Info"), *Typisch ich* ("Typical Me") and *Lernbörse* ("Learning Bourse"). Different websites target different segments of the population, such as young people, people interested in vocational training and occupations, employed individuals who want to advance their skills and the general public (OECD, 2021[1]).

The SenIAS also operates the Berlin-specific *Berliner Weiterbildungsdatenbank* ("CET Database Berlin"; WDB). The database includes around 40 000 entries from approximately 1 100 adult education providers. It is updated daily. Its interface is easy to operate and only requires users to enter their postcode and the CET field in which they are interested. Users can also limit the geographical search distance to display offers in their vicinity. WDB's main focus is on professional development courses but it also includes a wide range of courses offered by the VHS on topics related to civil society, politics and culture. A cooperation exists between the WDB and the Brandenburg-specific similar database *Weiterbildung Brandenburg* ("Further education in Brandenburg"). In the main WDB search portal, the offers of both databases are displayed. WDB also offers generic links to general CET funding options for each course in the database. However, to increase take-up of these financial instruments, displayed funding options could be tailored to individual needs more precisely and links to required documents could be provided.

The WDB also offers further in-built services for companies and adult education providers but could. Companies can use WDB's interactive instruments to analyse the need for qualification within their own establishment. They can also send inquiries to adult learning providers to find suitable offers. Information on CET funding opportunities for companies are also available within WDB. However, feedback from social partners gathered by the OECD for the purposes of this report also revealed that employers often find it difficult to navigate the WDB. Future updates of the database could specifically address employers on the WDB's home page. Adult learning providers primarily use the platform to publish their offers, which they can then also cross-post in other CET databases such as the nationwide Kursnet.

Financial incentives for individuals

Financial incentives for individuals can take different forms but generally aim to remove financial constraints that hamper CET participation. The main forms of financial incentives offered to individuals are education allowances, loans at preferential rates, CET premiums, scholarships, CET subsidies, tax incentives and education vouchers (OECD, 2021[1]).

In 2020, the German federal government offered 10 such financial incentive schemes. The different programmes funded by the German federal government are summarised in Table 4.3. On the highest level, these can be distinguished by the type of policy instrument, their respective target group and the scope of the measure. Target groups are often narrowly defined and eligibility depends on a range of socio-economic characteristics such as the level of education, age, employment status and income. The scope of the measure refers to the type of training the programme supports.

Table 4.3. Different types of financial incentive schemes offered by the German federal government

Programme name	English translation	Type of instrument	Target group	Scope of CET
Aufwendungen für die Aus- und Fortbildung	CET expenses	Tax incentive	Tax payers participating in CET	Job-related training
Bildungskredit	Education loan	Loan	18-35 year olds	Vocational and higher CET, internships
Aktivierungs und Vermittlungsgutschein	Activation and counselling voucher	Voucher	Courses of occupational inclusion and activation	Job-related training
Bildungsgutschein	Education voucher	Voucher	Unemployed, persons threatened by unemployment or low educated	Jon-related training
Bildungsprämie	Education grant	Voucher	Low-income workers	Job-related specialist courses, interdisciplinary trainings (non-formal)
Aufstiegs-BAföG	Upgrading training assistance	Allowance	Adults with a IVET degree	Formal CET
Zukunftsstarter	Future starter	Allowance	25-35 year olds without IVET degree and/or in low-skilled jobs	IVET
Aufstiegsstipendium	Advancement stipend	Scholarship	Adults with initial vocational qualification and work experience	Academic studies
Weiterbildungsstipendium	CET stipend	Scholarship	Graduates of initial vocational training; <25 years old	Specialist courses, interdisciplinary training, higher education courses
Weiterbildungsprämie	CET premium	Premium	Unemployed individuals	Formal CET courses of >2 years

Source: Summary table based on (OECD, 2021[1])

The wide range of financial incentive instruments allows for targeting specific segments of the population but bears risks of low take-up. The first potential issue is that individuals may find it hard to navigate through the different offers and are unlikely to be aware of all the different funding options. The second risk pertains to the narrowly defined target groups and type of CET covered. Without an overarching framework, such specific targeting may lead to some individuals "falling through the cracks". For example, earlier OECD work notes that individuals who find their skills and qualifications to become less relevant in the labour market do not have options to upgrade their skills on their own initiative but have to rely on government measures targeted at employers (OECD, 2021[1]). Box 4.6 describes the two new laws that govern these financial support options for employers – the *Qualifizierungschancengesetz* (Skills Development Opportunities Act") and the *Arbeit-von-morgen-Gesetz* ("Work of Tomorrow Act") – in detail.

The German federal states further complement these financial incentives according to regional needs, but Berlin did not offer additional financial incentives to individuals before the COVID-19 pandemic started. In 2019, 10 out of 16 German federal states offered additional vouchers covering direct costs for job-related CET. The target group of these additional offers were mostly low-educated and low-income individuals, as well as employees and owners of small and micro enterprises (OECD, 2021[1]). However, some measures also target the development of specific skills. One example includes the "Bavarian education cheque", a programme that ran until July 2021. It was supported by the European Social Fund and paid EUR 500 to employees who aimed to develop their digital skills in training courses that last a minimum of 8 hours (Bayerischen Staatsministeriums für Familie, 2021[16]). In addition to education vouchers, 8 out of 16 federal states offered CET premiums for formal vocational upskilling qualifications in 2019 (OECD, 2021[1]).

In response to the COVID-19 pandemic, Berlin's SenIAS introduced a CET premium for workers who were forced to reduce their working hours during the pandemic. Like other OECD countries, Germany introduced a job retention scheme in the form of short-time work (*Kurzarbeit*) to contain the employment fallout caused by the COVID-19 pandemic. Since March 2020, firms can request financial support from the federal government if 10% of their workforce are affected by cuts in working hours. Public employment services reimburse employers for these reductions in working hours while employees continue to receive parts of their salaries for hours they do not work (OECD, 2021[17]). To encourage uptake of education and training among affected employees, the SenIAS introduced an additional premium. Employees working reduced hours receive EUR 250 monthly if they participate in education or training measures every day of the month. Longer or shorter training courses are supported proportionally against this benchmark. Only courses offered by the BA Berlin-Brandenburg are eligible for support (Senatsverwaltung für Integration Arbeit und Soziales, 2021[18]).

Due to the high share of own-account workers in Berlin compared to other German regions and cities, they present a natural target group for city-level initiatives. As detailed above, both the share of self-employed in total employment and the share of own-account workers among the self-employed are higher in Berlin than in other German cities and regions. Across the OECD, CET among own-account workers are supported through five main instruments: Tax deductions, subsidies, financial incentives, wage replacement schemes and employment insurance plans (OECD, 2019[11]). Box 4.5 provides an example from Vienna, Austria, where training is financed for some own-account workers.

Box 4.5. The Waff training account – education and training options for own-account workers in Vienna, Austria

While support schemes are typically implemented by national governments, some city-level initiatives exist that also target own-account workers. In Vienna, Austria, the **Waff Training Account** provides training grants to certain own-account workers who have their business license or their main residence in Vienna, are in possession of a valid trade license, are insured under the Commercial Social Security Act and do not employ any employees.

Waff funds training and further education aimed at expanding entrepreneurial skills and training to improve commercial and business skills. The latter include courses in the areas of accounting, controlling, office organization or time management. Courses to acquire and improve digital skills are also funded. These include courses in the areas of social media, Photoshop, ICDL or e-billing. Finally, Waff also funds language courses such as business English or business German. Formal education that leads to degrees is not covered.

Waff covers 80% of the total training costs, up to a maximum of EUR 2 000. There is no limit on the number of courses that can be attended until the maximum coverage is reached. To ease facilitation, applications can be submitted before the training course begins up until four weeks after the start date of the course.

Source: OECD (2019[11]), *OECD Employment Outlook 2019: The Future of Work*; Waff (2021[19]), *Weiterbildungsförderung für Ein-Personen-Unternehmen (EPU)*.

Educational leave law

The educational leave law in Berlin is generous compared to other German federal states. Educational leave laws are a competence of the German federal states and allow employees to take leave from work for educational purposes. All but two federal states have such educational leave laws. Table 4.4 shows the generosity of these measures by German federal states. Most states offer employees five days of educational leave per year. Berlin's model of offering 10 days per two years adds some flexibility to the generic model. Under the law, educational leave is granted for job-related training and political education. Political education is understood as a broad term that covers general adult education on broader societal issues.

Table 4.4. The generosity of educational leave laws across German federal states

Federal State	Educational leave law	Paid leave	Reimbursement of wages for employers	Duration of leave
Baden-Württemberg	Yes	Yes	No	5 days per year, cannot be cumulated
Bayern	No	–	–	–
Berlin	Yes	Yes	No	10 days per 2 years
Brandenburg	Yes	Yes	No	10 days per 2 years; accumulation of leave entitlements possible based on written agreement between employer and employee
Bremen	Yes	Yes	No	10 days per 2 years
Hamburg	Yes	Yes	No	10 days per 2 years
Hessen	Yes	Yes	Enterprises with <20 employees can request wage subsidy of 50% for job-related CET and civic education; all enterprises can request 100% wage subsidy for training courses for the purpose of voluntary work (*Ehrenamt*)	5 days per year, can be cumulated over two years
Mecklenburg-Vorpommern	Yes	Yes	Enterprises can request EUR 55-110 wage subsidy per day	5 days per year, cannot be cumulated
Niedersachsen	Yes	Yes	No	5 days per year, can be cumulated over 4 years
Nordrhein-Westfalen	Yes	Yes	No	5 days per year, can be cumulated over 2 years
Rheinland-Pfalz	Yes	Yes	Enterprises with <50 employees can request wage subsidy of 50% of average salary in the Federal State	10 days per 2 years
Saarland	Yes	Yes		2 days + 4 half days per year
Sachsen	No	–	–	–
Schleswig-Holstein	Yes	Yes		5 days per year, can be cumulated over 2 years
Sachsen-Anhalt	Yes	Yes		5 days per year, can be cumulated over 2 years
Thüringen	Yes	Yes		5 days per year, can be cumulated over two years if rejected

Note: The new *Berliner Bildungszeitgesetz* ("Berlin educational leave law") came into effect on September 1, 2021.
Source: Overview for federal states based on (OECD, 2021, p. 129[1]) with additions from *Berliner Bildungszeitgesetz* (BiZeitG; "Berlin educational leave law", version July 5, 2021).

Participation in educational leave remains relatively low in Berlin, but a slight upward trend is visible over the past decade. In 2018, the latest year for which complete data is available, 16 520 employees in Berlin took educational leave. This corresponds to approximately 1% of the underlying eligible population. In absolute terms, the number of educational leave takers thus increased significantly compared to the year 2010, when 9 834 took advantage of this measure. However, as the size of the labour force also grew over the same time period, the relative number of participants only increased marginally (Figure 4.7).

The vast majority of employees taking educational leave did so to pursue work-related training. In 2018, 85% of educational leave takers pursued work-related training. Around 10% took time off work to take courses on political education. Another 5% of educational leave takers engaged in a combination of both types of CET.

Figure 4.7. The total number of educational leave takers in Berlin is growing slowly over the years

Total number of educational leave takers and educational leave takers as a share of social security contributing employees in Berlin, 2010 to 2019

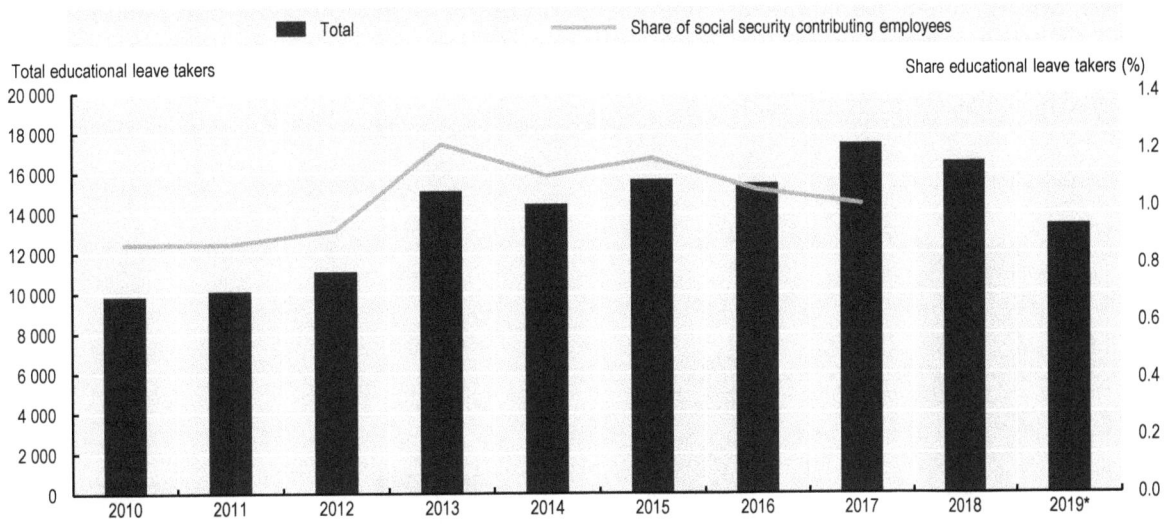

Note: Data on the share of educational leave takers not yet available for years following 2017.
* Data reporting for the year 2019 is incomplete and likely to be revised upward.
Source: OECD illustration based on data provided by SenIAS.

Women in Berlin are more likely to take educational leave than men. The data shown in Figure 4.7 can be further disaggregated by gender and the level of education. In 2018, 57% of educational leave takers were female, a continuation of a historical trend. Since 1991, women constituted more than 50% of educational leave takers in every recorded year.

Individuals without professional qualification constitute a negligible share of educational leave takers. Only 7% of employees taking time off work for educational purposes did not hold any professional qualification. EU-LFS data shows that the share of Berlin's labour force without professional qualification (a level of education below upper secondary education) among 25 to 64 year olds stood at 12.9% in 2018. Thus, low-educated individuals are underrepresented among those who take educational leave, even though they are among the groups to benefit the most from additional training or education.

Financial incentives for companies

Companies in Berlin stress the importance of financial incentives for expanding their CET offers. Figure 4.8 shows that 73% of Berlin-based companies surveyed by the IHK respond that financial support would be the most useful type of support to help them expand their in-house CET. 52% of companies state that greater flexibility of financial support by the government would be helpful. Access to information on CET offers and support in CET planning are further reasons mentioned by 30% and 29% of surveyed companies respectively.

The German federal government does offer generous financial incentives to increase CET in small companies. The German federal government has recently passed two new laws, the *Qualifizierungschancengesetz* ("Skills Development Opportunities Act") and the *Arbeit-von-morgen-Gesetz* ("Work of Tomorrow Act") that support companies in their efforts to offer CET to employees. The amount of the subsidy depends on a range of parameters such as the size of the company, the share of workers within the company who require training, the type of CET offered and the education level and work experience of participants. Very small companies can get up to 100% of their incurred direct and indirect cost reimbursed. Box 4.6 describes these laws in more detail.

Figure 4.8. Enterprises in Berlin declare financial support the main type of support needed to expand CET within the company

Self-declared by companies surveyed, 2021

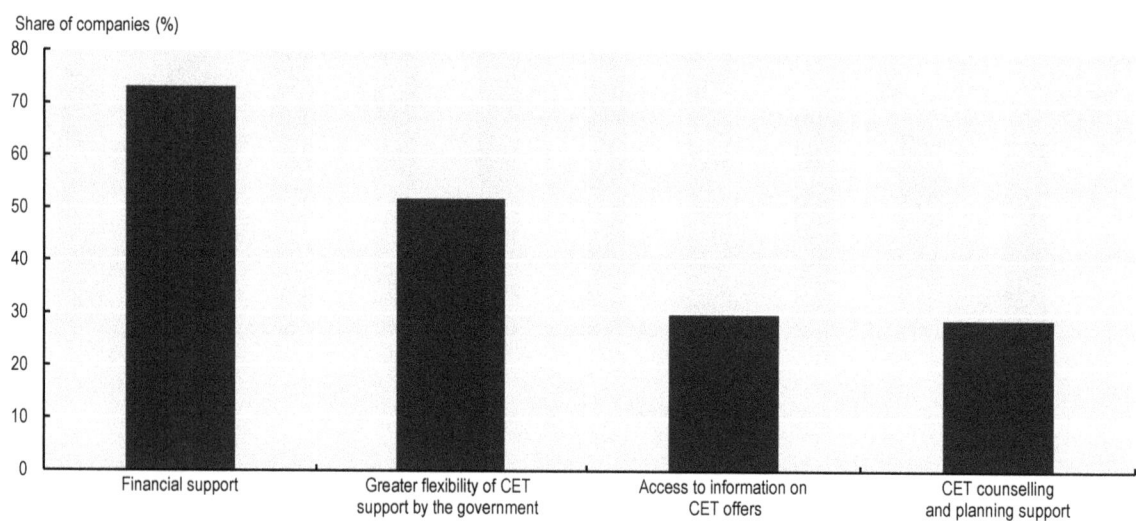

Note: Based on a sample of 560 companies.
Source: Chamber of Commerce and Industry of Berlin (IHK Berlin), *Sommerumfrage 2021* ("summer survey 2021").

Unlike other federal states, Berlin does not offer additional financial incentives to companies to improve CET participation. In Germany, 13 out of 16 federal states complement the instruments provided by the federal government (OECD, 2021[1]). Some of these measures predate the new instruments laid out in the Skills Development Opportunities Act and the Work of Tomorrow Act and are therefore likely to be phased out. However, some of these complementary initiatives fill important gaps: For example, federal states generally support education and training opportunities without any lower limit on their duration. Therefore, they add some flexibility to measures funded under the countrywide Skills Development Opportunities Act and the Work of Tomorrow Act, where the minimum course duration is three weeks to be eligible for funding. Measures on the federal state level are often co-funded by the European Social Fund (ESF) (OECD, 2021[1]).

> **Box 4.6. Germany has recently introduced two new laws that strengthen financial support for training and education measures offered by SMEs**
>
> **Skills Development Opportunities Act**
>
> The *Qualifizierungschancengesetz* ("Skills Development Opportunities Act") came into effect in January 2019. It is part of the German national training strategy and replaces the 2006-2019 WeGebAU Programme, under which subsidies were granted to SMEs. The WeGebAU Programme specifically targeted older workers and adults with low levels of education. The primary aim of the new Skills Development Opportunities Act is to widen access to subsidised training opportunities for all workers if these are affected by structural change or work in professions characterised by a shortage of skilled workers (*Engpassberuf*). Under the new law, CET measures can be subsidised if the training lasts for at least four weeks and the participating worker has at least three years of work experience.
>
> The amount of the subsidy depends on the size of the company, the share of workers within the company who require training, the type of CET offered and the education level and work experience of participants. Both part-time and full-time training options are supported as long as the minimum training duration is met.
>
> *Direct* training costs of CET offered within SMEs with fewer than 10 employees, training for workers above the age of 45 and training for low-educated workers are fully covered. Large companies of more than 2500 employees can only claim up to 20% of the training costs, reflecting their higher ability and willingness to offer training in-house.
>
> *Indirect* training costs, i.e. wage costs accruing to the employer while workers are undergoing training measures, are also covered. Cost coverage rates again depend on a range of parameters similar to those of the direct training costs. In SMEs with fewer than 10 employees, between 75% (the baseline) and 100% of wage costs can be claimed, depending on the education level of the participating employee. In larger SMEs up to 250 employees, between 50% (the baseline) and 100% of the wage costs are covered, depending on the education level of the participating employee.
>
> **Work of Tomorrow Act**
>
> The *Arbeit-von-morgen-Gesetz* ("Work of Tomorrow Act") builds on the Skills Development Opportunities Act and expands on some details. The law came into effect in October 2020. It increases some of the subsidies offered to companies that are affected by structural change. Most importantly, it reduces the minimum duration of training measures eligible for subsidies from four to three weeks. It also increases funding for training by ten percentage points if at least every fifth employee in a company needs further training. For SMEs that employ more than 10 and fewer than 250 employees the ten percentage point increase only requires 10% of employees to be in need for training.
>
> Source: OECD (2021[1]), *Continuing Education and Training in Germany*.

However, early data for the whole of Germany shows that the take-up of these new measures remains low, in particular among the smallest SMEs. A survey conducted by the BA in October/November 2020 suggests that only one in ten German companies make use of the new financial instruments that aim to support CET. Among surveyed companies that employ fewer than 10 employees, only 26% were aware of the new instruments, compared to 67% of companies that employ more than 250 employees. Only 6% of the smallest companies had made use of the financial support measures, compared to 35% among large companies. Companies that employ between 11 and 250 employees fell in between these extremes on both metrics (Institute for Employment Research, 2021[20]).

Employers name five reasons for the low-take up of financial support to increase CET offers. Fifty-three percent of German companies that were aware of the CET financial support options but did not make use of them responded not having found suitable CET courses and programmes for their employees. 37% responded that the administrative burden was too high, 34% responded refused to engage with the BA, 30% of the surveyed companies responded that their employees were not interested in CET and 27% responded that the minimum duration to become eligible for financial support was too long (Institute for Employment Research, 2021[20]). Taken together, a lack of awareness among small employers in particular and the lack of (human) resources to navigate through offers appear to be the major bottlenecks that hamper take-up.

Despite the low take-up of financial support measures, employers in Berlin continue to attach importance to CET, with a rising need for digital skill development. Figure 4.9 shows that the overall importance of CET for employers has approximately stayed constant. However, some CET content have gained importance among employers, while the development of some other skills has become less relevant. For example, the share of employers that named digital skills and the ability to adapt to digitalisation has increased by 16 and 13 percentage points respectively between 2016 (2017) and 2019. On the other hand, the share of employers that named business specific skills as a particular important CET topic dropped by 16 percentage points over the same period. The development of other skills, such as project management and the ability to speak foreign languages, has stayed constant. Taken together, the findings imply that Berlin's employers acknowledge the increasing importance of skills that allow employees to adapt to a changing labour market.

Figure 4.9. Employers in Berlin increasingly attach importance to digital skills training

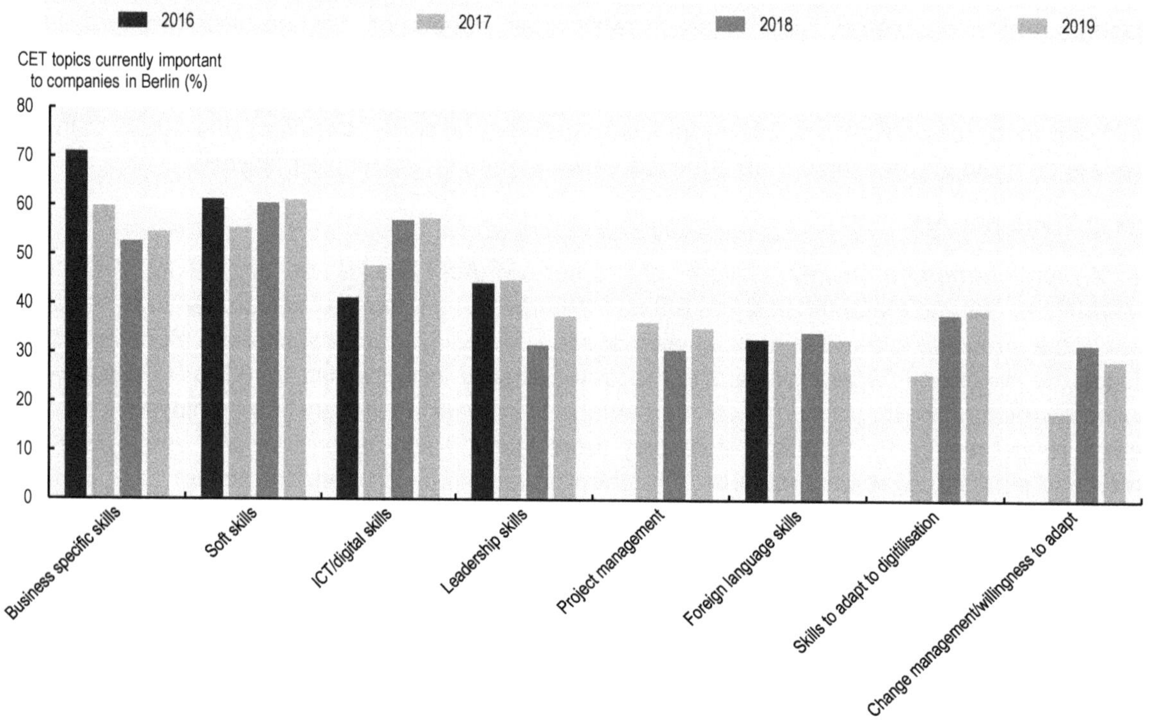

Note: Sample size differs between years. N(2016)=436; N(2017)=480; N(2018)=335; N(2019)=223.
Source: Chamber of Commerce and Industry (IHK) Berlin - Education and Further Education survey

To engage Berlin's SMEs in local skill development, innovative solutions are needed. The analysis in this chapter suggests that financial support is important but by itself often insufficient to increase training and education offers in SMEs. At the same time, the need for updating and upgrading employees' skills within SMEs according to structural labour market changes is evident. Other cities across the OECD have therefore started to acknowledge the need to go beyond financial incentives. For example, the city of Vantaa, Finland, has started to contact SMEs proactively. Training programmes are then developed jointly with SMEs. Box 4.7 describes the approach taken by the city of Vantaa in more detail.

Box 4.7. Supporting growth and social investments in SMEs through skill development in Vantaa, Finland

The city of Vantaa, the fourth biggest city of Finland, has identified the need to develop a new model to support education and training in SMEs.

The Urban Growth Vantaa project brings together relevant city departments, education providers, research institutes and businesses in Vantaa to develop a local jobs and skills ecosystem with the aim to support both local SMEs and their employees in employment, upskilling and digitalization. The primary target group of the initiatives are low-educated adults employed by SMEs who do not traditionally fall into the category of continuous learners. This specific group is often at risk of job loss due to the automation of production processes. A second target group are executives of SMEs who aim to grow their company responsibly.

Employees in SMEs are typically supported through a **co-created apprenticeship services programme**. These apprenticeships are targeted at individuals as an opportunity to earn a vocational degree. Urban Growth Vantaa's solution is to contact companies to introduce training ideas and their benefits to SME decision makers and employees simultaneously. In a first step, SMEs with 10-200 employees are contacted by the project coordinators. SMEs then undergo a needs assessment to identify skill needs through surveys. SMEs are then informed of the different CET options that could develop these relevant skills. A discussion with the individual employees then follows and an appropriate apprenticeship is identified for them. The apprenticeships are free of charge for employees and SME continue to pay their full salaries. If the reduction in working hours at full salary cannot be borne by SMEs, financial support schemes exist.

Alternatively, employees of SMEs can be trained in a so-called **growth-coaching programme**. The programme follows a similar structure but takes a forward-looking approach. Business development needs are identified in consultation with SME executives and employees then undergo the appropriate training to meet these needs.

The Urban Growth Vantaa project further acknowledges resource constraints faced by SMEs and introduces the idea of a "one-stop-shop". To this end, the project assigns a **project account manager** to each SME who coordinates CET efforts with a company representative.

The European Regional Development Fund (ERDF) granted approximately EUR 4 million in funding for the project. The project has thus far reached 70 SMEs and provided training or support to 714 adults. It initially runs from January 2019 to April 2022.

Source: Urban Innovative Actions Initiative (2021[21]), *Urban Growth-GSIP Vantaa - Growth and Social investment Pacts for Local Companies in the City of Vantaa*.

In response to the resource constraints SMEs face, so-called *Weiterbildungsverbünde* ("CET employers' networks") have recently started to develop in Berlin. Initiated by the German Federal Ministry of Labour and Social Affairs (BMAS) as part of the *Nationale Weiterbildungsstrategie* ("National Skills Strategy"; NWS) in 2021, CET employers' networks aim to bring together local companies, actors from the wider CET training landscape, as well as regional labour market actors. They aim to develop and organise joint training measures that can be carried out across company boundaries in a resource-saving manner. The focus is in particular on the exchange between the partners of a network, the identification of further training needs in participating companies as well as advice on and research for suitable further training offers. Four of such employers' networks in Berlin have started receiving funding from BMAS. Table 4.5 provides an overview of the networks. The funding covers up to 70% of costs incurred by these networks, up to a maximum of EUR 1 million for 36 months (Bundesministerium für Arbeit und Soziales, 2021[22]).

Two of these CET employers' networks explicitly focus on developing training measures that improve digital skills and respond to newly arising skills needs in light of the automation of production processes. Both the *Netzwerk Großbeerenstraße* and the *R-Learning Kollektiv* plan to put their emphasis on creating courses that help their members advance the digital skills of their employees.

The success of CET employers' networks will depend on how well they manage to integrate SMEs that have not offered training and education to employees so far. To this end, the city of Berlin could support the participation of very small companies in the networks. SenIAS could track developments closely within networks such as the *Netzwerk Großbeerenstraße*, for which it serves as a partner. To develop networks further and beyond the initial funding period, the city of Berlin could follow the suggestions put forward by the *Bundesvereinigung der Deutschen Arbeitgeberverbände* ("Confederation of German Employers' Associations"; BDA). The BDA proposes to engage large companies in such networks. These could open their training courses and workshops outside of regular operating hours, and with their expertise, they could offer advanced training on new machines and technologies for employees of SMEs (Bundesvereinigung der Deutschen Arbeitgeberverbände, 2021[23]). SenIAS could take over the coordination of their engagement in the long-term.

Table 4.5. CET employers' networks in Berlin

Original name	English name	Actors involved	Focus
Modellhafte Etablierung einer Koordinierungs-stelle für den Aufbau eines Weiterbildungsverbundes im Automotive-Cluster Berlin-Brandenburg (MEKA-BB)	Pilot coordination office for the development of a CET network in the automotive cluster Berlin-Brandenburg	Association for Vocational Education Research e.V. (IBBF); Society for the Promotion of Educational Research and Qualification GmbH (GEBIFO); Centre for vocational and continuous education GmbH Ludwigsfelde-Luckenwalde	Automotive
HOGA.Co	HOGA.Co	bildungsmarkt e.v., Dehoga, Food and Catering Trade Union NGG, IHK	Hospitality industry
R-Learning Kollektiv	R-Learning Collective	GFBM Akademie gGmbH; ITS mobility GmbH; ABB VET centre Berlin; Berufsbildungsverein Prenzlau	Control technology, digitalisation and automation
Weiterbildungsverbund der Berlin-Brandenburger Unternehmensnetzwerke (WBV)	CET network of the enterprises in Berlin-Brandenburg	Netzwerk Großbeerenstraße e.V.	Digitalisation, sustainability, artificial intelligence, quality of training and intercultural organisational development

Source: OECD (2022[15]).

Increasing participation in CET among vulnerable population groups for a better labour market integration

A better integration of Berlin's strong adult education centres as a place of CET and career guidance into the local CET ecosystem could benefit migrants in particular

Ranked by hours of education offered per capita, Berlin has one of the strongest VHS systems in Germany. Figure 4.10 shows the number of VHS courses offered per 1 000 residents in Berlin (Panel A) and the hours of education and training offered within Berlin's VHS per 1 000 residents (Panel B) in 2019. While the number of VHS courses offered is around the median when compared to German federal states, the 243 hours of education and training offered by Berlin's VHS per 1 000 residents is third only to the federal states of Niedersachsen and Baden-Württemberg that offered 282 and 262 hours of course work per 1 000 residents respectively. The two metrics combined suggest that VHS in Berlin offer mostly training and education of relatively longer duration compared to other German federal states.

Figure 4.10. VHS offers in Berlin are generous compared to other German federal states

Number of courses per 1 000 residents (Panel A) and number of hours of education per 1 000 residents (Panel B) in 2019

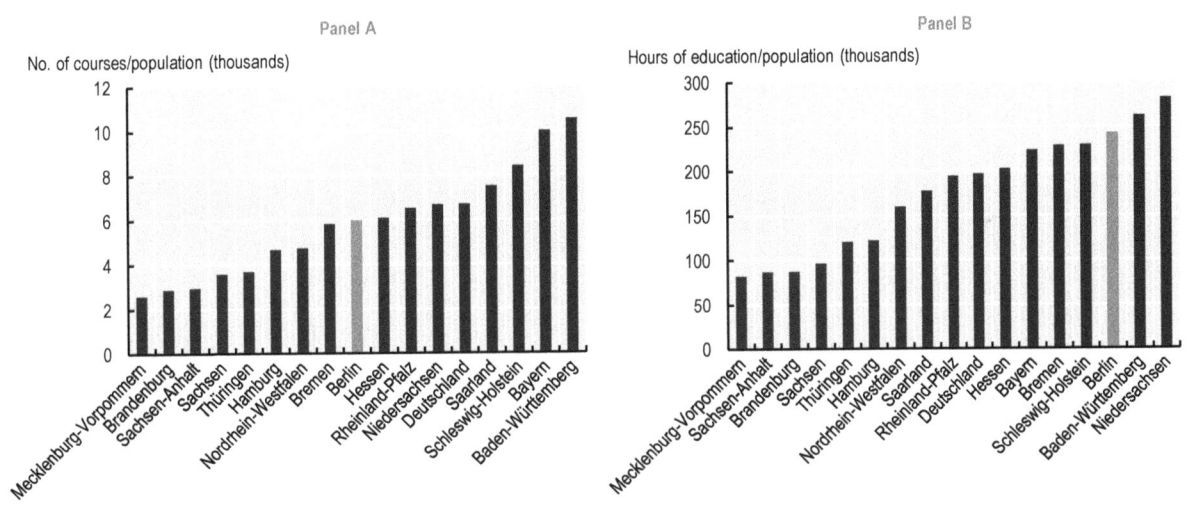

Source: OECD calculation based on Huntemann et al. (2019[24]).

A striking feature of CET offered by the VHS in Berlin is the large amount of language courses. Figure 4.11 shows that the explanation for the relatively long duration of courses in Berlin's VHS lies in the relatively large share of language courses in the total amount of courses offered. In 2019, 50.4% of courses offered in Berlin's VHS were language courses, compared to 32.3% on average across all German federal states. Language courses require relatively more hours of teaching than courses on other commonly taught topics such as health or culture. Courses on health and culture made up 18.1% and 16.3% of total courses offered in Berlin in 2019, compared to 34.7% and 15.9% respectively for Germany as a whole. In the same year, job-related training in the fields of IT and management only made up 9.2% of the total number of courses in Berlin (Germany as a whole: 8.1%).

The majority of these language courses offered by VHS are German language courses. While no data exists on Berlin specifically, 68% of language courses offered by VHS in Germany as a whole in 2019 were German language courses. Of these, 53% were offered within integration courses financed by the

Bundesamt für Migration und Flüchtlinge ("Federal Office for Migration and Refugees"). These integration courses are sometimes compulsory for migrants who do not speak basic German. Both the Job Centers (if the migrant receives social assistance) and the *Landesamt für Einwanderung* ("Berlin Immigration Office") can place migrants under the obligation to participate.

However, while many migrants use VHS German language courses for integration into the German society, VHS in Berlin do not currently offer guidance on labour market integration. One of the striking observations in Figure 4.12 is the job market counselling offered by VHS in Hessen compared to other German federal states, with Berlin, Bremen, Mecklenburg-Vorpommern, Sachsen and Sachsen-Anhalt not offering labour market guidance at all. While limited in scope, such offers exist in VHS in other German federal states. Most noteworthy, in the federal state of Hessen, more than 35 000 people received job market counselling in VHS. These counselling efforts in Hessen are partly financed by the *Hessischer Weiterbildungspakt* ("Hessen covenant on further education"), an initiative by the federal state of Hessen to strengthen its CET system. Based on existing projects, the VHS in Frankfurt am Main, Wiesbaden and Groß-Gerau developed a best-practice guide on CET and professional guidance. One example on labour market guidance offered to migrants is described in more detail in Box 4.8.

Figure 4.11. More than half of the courses offered by Berlin's VHS are language courses

Share of courses offered by Adult Education Centres across German federal states in 2019, by topic

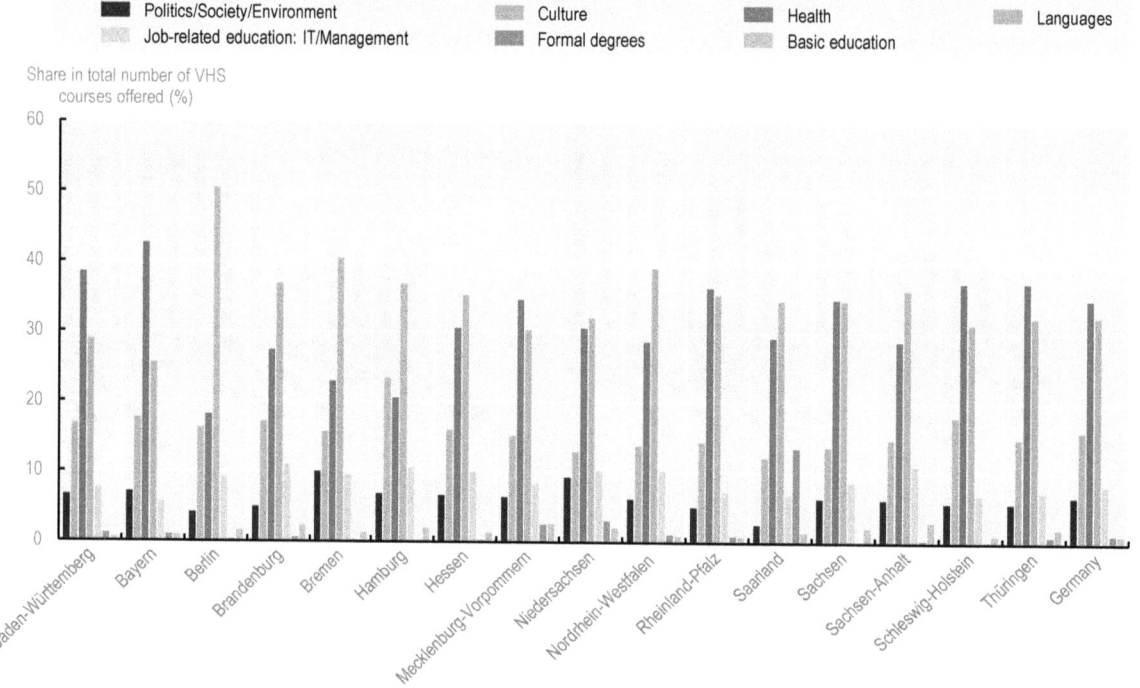

Source: OECD calculation based on Huntemann et al. (2019[24])

Figure 4.12. Berlin's VHS do not currently offer counselling on labour market integration

Total number of persons receiving counselling on labour market integration in 2019

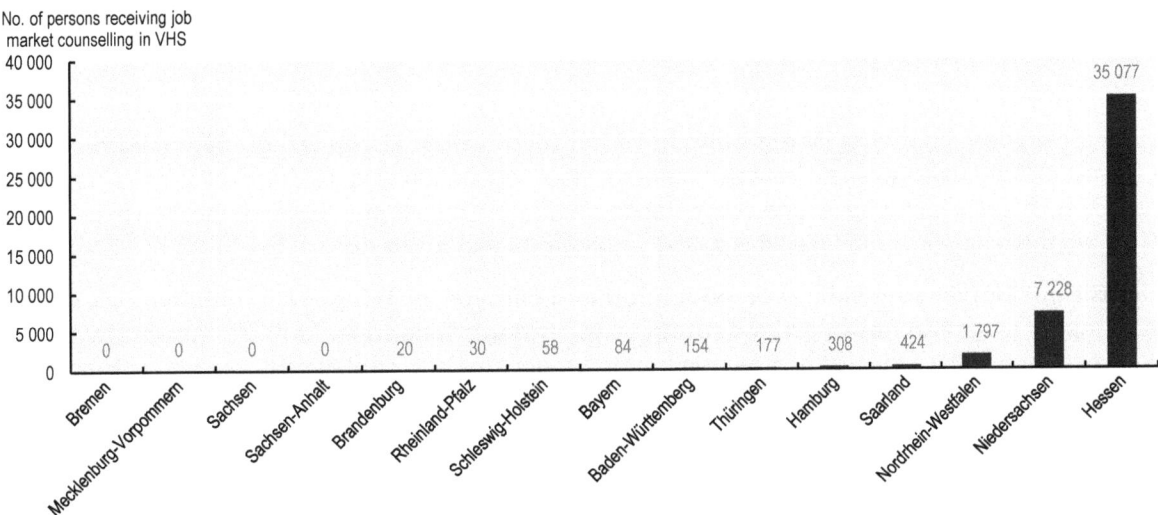

Source: OECD elaboration on Huntemann et al. (2019[24]).

Box 4.8. Labour market counselling for migrants at the VHS Wiesbaden, Hessen

In 2020, three VHS based in Frankfurt am Main, Wiesbaden and Groß-Gerau created a best-practice guide in order to collect experiences and findings from the project *VHS – Ort für Bildung und Beratung* ("VHS – a place for education and counselling") funded by the Hessian government's covenant on further education. The objective of the guide is to derive recommendations for action for all VHS in Hessen and Germany that would like to develop their counselling services.

One of these best-practice examples from the VHS Wiesbaden lays out in detail how migrants who participate in German language courses at VHS can benefit from guidance services without the creation of a competing institution. Two key pillars serve as the foundation of the approach.

The first pillar is to leverage existing VHS structures and build on these. In Wiesbaden, the HESSENCAMPUS Wiesbaden, which is institutionally affiliated to the VHS Department of Occupations and Careers, already offered career counselling services as part of their guidance on further education. This generic guidance open to anyone includes guidance on professional development, re-integration into the labour market after a career break, CET, initial education, skill analyses, tertiary education, education support schemes and writing job applications. The new initiative expanded this generic career counselling to include migrant-specific guidance on the recognition of foreign degrees, general information on the German education system, vocational training in Germany and entering the German labour market, the link between the residence permit and the labour market and guidance on the importance of language skills.

The second pillar is to draw on existing networks and build new partnerships to ensure cross-institutional synergies. The key advantage of the VHS is that their target group, i.e. migrants who either are obliged to or voluntarily take part in German language courses, is already present. However, the guidance offered in the VHS does not replicate existing offers. The *HESSENCAMPUS Wiesbaden* offers a point of first contact to assess needs and connects participants to relevant institutions such as

> schools, local Job Centers or the BA. These networks also include migrant-specific institutional contact points that can support migrants in matters such as the recognition of foreign degrees.
>
> Source: OECD summary based on Volkshochschule Frankfurt am Main (2020[25]), *Praxisordner Beratung - Themen, Vorgehensweisen, Erfahrungen.*

Two main reasons exist why Berlin does not offer labour market related guidance within its VHS. First, Berlin strictly distinguishes between general adult education and job-market related training and education, with each falling under the competence of different ministries. Second, as shown in Table 4.2, the CET guidance landscape in Berlin is already numerous and scattered.

The MoBiBe ("Mobile counselling on education and careers for refugees") initiative has started to fill this gap by targeting newly-arrived refugees in strategic locations. MoBiBe, initiated by SenIAS in 2015 in response to the arrival of a large number of asylum seekers, strategically positions its mobile units near sites that host or teach refugees, including the VHS. To give mobile units visibility, MoBiBe staff members also introduce their counselling services during German language courses (Senatsverwaltung für Integration, 2015[26]).

While promising, operations of MoBiBe are still relatively limited and could be scaled up to include all migrants. In total, MoBiBe held 8 447 counselling sessions in 2019, with 5 552 individuals receiving counselling. In comparison, the job market counselling offered by VHS in Hessen reached 35 077 individuals in the same year (Figure 4.12). Hessen's total population in 2019 stood at 6.3 million, compared to 3.6 million in Berlin. The share of population with a migration background is on a similar level in the two federal states (Berlin: 33.1% in 2019; Hessen: 34.4% in 2019). While generally open to other migrant groups, MoBiBe currently tailors its counselling services mostly to refugees. This is reflected in the country of origin of individuals receiving counselling. In 2019, the majority of individuals receiving counselling were Syrians (20.4%), Iranians (12.4%) and Afghans (9.6%) (Senatsverwaltung für Integration Arbeit und Soziales, 2020[27]). A natural option to scale up the promising work of MoBiBe is to extend it to people with a migration background that are not recent refugees.

Promising innovative initiatives targeting vulnerable segments of the population involve social economy actors

Berlin has an active social economy that supports and complements adult learning measures by the PES, the federal government, and the federal state government. The OECD defines the social economy as the set of organisations and associations that are driven by "values of solidarity, the primacy of people over capital, and democratic and participative governance" (OECD, 2021[28]). Experiences from across the OECD show that social economy initiatives can reinforce local development approaches by national, regional and local governments (OECD, 2020[29]). In Berlin, some initiatives in the field of CET complement the government measures discussed throughout the previous sections of this chapter. Two of them, the *Grundbildungszentrum Berlin* ("Berlin Centre for Basic Education") and the *ReDI School of Digital Integration* are discussed in more detail in the following.

The Berlin Centre for Basic Education targets functionally illiterate adults. A 2018 study by the University of Hamburg showed that 12.1% all adults in Germany struggle to extract the meaning from a basic text and/or are not able to write such texts. Among these adults, 62% were part of the labour force, 53% were native German speakers and 78% had completed at least mandatory schooling. While no statistics on adult illiteracy exist for Berlin explicitly, its relatively low labour force participation rate, its large share of foreign-born individuals and its relatively large share of early school leavers suggests that the share of adults who fall into the category of functionally illiterate adults could be even higher than the German average. The Berlin Centre for Basic Education targets these functionally illiterate adults by serving as a point of first contact, offering guidance events and individual counselling. Its *Grundbildungs-Atlas* ("basic education atlas") is a compilation of all Berlin learning and consulting offers and is available both offline and online (Berlin Centre for Basic Education, 2019[30]). The Berlin Centre for Basic Education is a cooperation of two NGOs that focus on basic education and adult literacy. The SenBJF provides financial support.

The Berlin Centre for Basic Education's promising "alpha label" initiative raises awareness of (functional) illiteracy among adults and could be scaled up across Berlin. The alpha label is a label for institutions and organisation in Berlin. It signals that the services provided within a specific building or facility are accessible to adults with low-literacy. Obtaining the label requires staff training and equipping buildings and facilities with easy-to-read signs. Box 4.9 describes the alpha label in more detail. The alpha label reduces the stigma of illiteracy by teaching staff of public institutions and social economy organisations how to guide adults with low literacy towards existing education and training offers. It thereby promotes basic education in Berlin and serves as a valuable tool to approach segments of the population that are otherwise difficult to reach.

Box 4.9. Berlin's "alpha label" to facilitate basic education and social inclusion

Since 2016, a specific quality label exists for institutions and organisations that offer their services in a way easily accessible to adults with low literacy. To receive the label, at least 20% of an institution's or organisation's employees need to take part in a half-day awareness workshop and all communication channels such as websites need to be accessible to readers with low literacy. Within the physical space of an organisation or institution that is open to the public, easy-to-read signs need to be visible. The development of the label, as well as support for providers during its adaptation period are supported by Berlin's Basic Education Centre and SenBJF.

As of 2019, about 70 Berlin-based institutions and organisations were in the process of obtaining the label and more than 30 organizations had already obtained it. The latter includes all basic education and literacy guidance providers, as well as Berlin's Agency for Civic Education, Berlin's Job Centers and several health care providers.

Source: OECD (2022[15]), *Career guidance for low-qualified workers in Germany (forthcoming)*; Berlin Centre for Basic Education (2019[30]), *Das Berliner Grund-Bildungs-Zentrum: Fortschritt und Stand*.

The ReDI School of Digital Integration targets refugees and teaches course participants advanced coding and programming skills. ReDI School offers a range of course options in coding and programming to refugees free of charge. These courses include courses on frontend web development, data science, software development as well as more software specific courses on Salesforce or Azure. Its offers are open to a wide range of refugees. It specifically caters some of its coding offers to women within its *digital women programme*, which provides childcare during the duration of courses and also offers interpretation in the classroom to encourage participation among women who do not speak English or German. Consequently, women make up 60% of its course participants. Further offers also include programmes for children aged 9 and above and youth aged 17 and above. Seventy-five percent of those graduating from ReDI Digital Career Program, its core module, currently have paid jobs, mostly in the technology industry. Box 4.10 provides more information on ReDI School's business model.

> **Box 4.10. Teaching migrants coding and programming: The ReDI School of digital integration**
>
> Since 2016, the ReDI School of Digital Integration provides refugees with free technological education in coding and fundamental computer training, at no cost and by experts. ReDI School's core objective is to help students become independent by teaching them digital skills. A network of tech leaders, students, and alumni assists in the creation of labour market opportunities for graduates of its programmes.
>
> The ReDI School teaches refugees cutting-edge IT skills to enter the technology sector. The state-of-the-art knowledge is taught by a network of more than 500 IT and start-up volunteers from more than 180 companies. Next to standard daytime offers, courses are also offered in the evenings and on weekends, adding flexibility for both teachers and potential students. The experts involved in the project also act as "door openers" by creating links between the students and the companies. Their role as teachers allows them to get to know the students and to understand their different motivations, interests and learning curves. Based on their industry knowledge, teachers then act as intermediaries by recommending students to companies that match their respective profiles.
>
> As of 2021, the number of applications is more than double the number of places available. Around 70% of the students who attend ReDI School's courses were recommended by friends or relatives, exemplifying the strong standing the ReDI School has in Berlin's migrant communities. Following its success in Berlin, the ReDI School has set up schools in Munich and North Rhine-Westphalia in Germany, as well as Copenhagen and Aarhus in Denmark. It also offers remote studying options.

The government of Berlin could ensure that the core business of the ReDI School is scaled up to include all migrants. So far, the ReDI School explicitly focusses on migrants who migrated to Berlin for humanitarian reasons and have obtained refugee status. The main reason for the limited focus are capacity and financial constraints. Berlin's SenIAS could ensure that the ReDI School's core business, i.e. the ReDI Digital Career Program, is sufficiently funded such that migrants who came for economic or family reasons can also join its courses.

Not requiring German skills to participate is a reason for the success of the ReDI School. Next to the minimum amount of bureaucracy required to join ReDI School's courses, digital skill training does not require German language skills. The ReDI School further directs its students to the BA for German language courses, which they can take in parallel.

Similar projects across the OECD combine vocational training with language training. Cities and regions of Sweden in particular have started implementing programmes that combine vocational and language training for migrants. Box 4.11 provides an overview of two promising initiatives.

> **Box 4.11. Combining language and vocational training for migrants – local initiatives in Sweden**
>
> **Yrkesväg Värmland**
>
> The Yrkesväg Värmland Project aims to address the difficulties in integrating into the labour market experienced by migrants and their families. In the Värmland region of Sweden, a large share of migrants lack the necessary education required for the regional labour market. Yrkesväg Värmland's main objective is to combine vocational training with language training.
>
> The project offers tailor-made courses for migrants by taking into account the education level of each person. It distinguishes between two target groups. The first group are newly arrived and long-term

unemployed foreign-born adults without secondary level education. The second group are foreign-born individuals with a level of education beyond secondary education. Both groups first receive a training course on health and human rights in Sweden. For the first group, the programme then offers two different course options, both running in parallel to Swedish language training. The first is a basic introduction to vocational training that includes an internship in a partner company. The second is a more profound vocational programme following a skill assessment. For the second, more educationally advanced group, workplace based learning opportunities are offered. The Yrkesväg Värmland Project is initially funded by the European Social Fund for a duration of two years, until June 2022.

The YFI and SFX programmes in Stockholm, Sweden

The city of Stockholm introduced two programmes to help migrants find work: The YFI (Integrated Swedish language and vocational training for migrants) and the SFX (Swedish language course for professionals) programme. The goal of both programmes is to give Swedish language lessons to newly-arrived migrants to facilitate their access to the labour market. The SFX programme targets migrants who already have a vocational background, while the YFI programme offers migrants without this background a combined vocational and language training.

Within the YFI programme provides students first study an introductory vocational course and Swedish classes for five to six months, with a focus on the vocabulary needed in the areas of their training in hospitality, construction and nursing. After the introductory course, migrants continue with a secondary level vocational education course, while continuing with their Swedish lessons. The collaboration between language teachers and vocational trainers is key to achieve high levels of engagement in these courses. Thanks to a partnership with the Swedish Public Employment Service, participants can do internships and work placements in the Stockholm region.

The SFX programme targets migrants with previous professional experience. Training offers are divided into 10 professional areas (bus drivers, truck drivers, entrepreneurs, craftsmen, engineers, architects, medical staff, teachers, programmers and healthcare professionals). The different training courses set different admission criteria based on age, previous work experience and education previously attained. Depending on the category a prospective student falls into, students are assigned to courses that differ in scope (full- or part-time and an estimation of teacher-led and self-study lessons) and in content. Internships and work placements are part of their curriculum. Students also take Swedish courses at different levels of proficiency.

The programmes are co-funded by the city of Stockholm, the European Social Fund and the European Union's Employment and Social Innovation Program.

Source: Yrkesväg Värmland (2021[31]), *Project presentation on Yrkesväg Värmland;* OECD (2021[32]), *STOCKHOLM, Sweden - The YFI and SFX Programmes to Support Migrants - Key facts: Content and mode of delivery.*

Berlin's VHS could implement such dual education approaches, but would have to be more open to integrate work-related courses into their curricula. Due to its importance in the provision of German language courses, the VHS are in a good position to expand its offers to combine these language courses with vocational training for migrants and refugees. Implementing such new programmes would explicitly call for increased cooperation with the BA to find suitable vocational training options and with employers' associations to arrange internships and work placements.

References

Bayerischen Staatsministeriums für Familie, A. (2021), "Bayerischer Bildungsscheck", https://www.stmas.bayern.de/arbeit/bildungsscheck/#sec1 (accessed on 4 January 2022). [16]

Berlin Centre for Basic Education (2019), "Das Berliner Grund-Bildungs-Zentrum: Fortschritt und Stand". [30]

Brunello, G. et al. (2020), *Financing Constraints and Employers' Investment in Training*, http://www.iza.org. [8]

Bundesministerium für Arbeit und Soziales (2021), *Das Bundesprogramm "Aufbau von Weiterbildungsverbünden"*, https://www.bmas.de/DE/Arbeit/Aus-und-Weiterbildung/Weiterbildungsrepublik/Weiterbildungsverbuende/weiterbildungsverbuende-art.html (accessed on 6 January 2022). [22]

Bundesvereinigung der Deutschen Arbeitgeberverbände (2021), *Den Strukturwandel der deutschen Wirtschaft klug und nachhaltig gestalten-gemeinsame Verantwortung von Wirtschaft, Sozialpartnern und Politik*. [23]

de la Roca, J. and D. Puga (2017), "Learning by Working in Big Cities", *The Review of Economic Studies*, Vol. 84/1, pp. 106-142, http://dx.doi.org/10.1093/RESTUD/RDW031. [5]

DIE and Bertelsmann Stiftung (2018), "Deutscher Weiterbildungsatlas. Teilnahme und Angebot in Kreisen und kreisfreien Städten". [7]

Dohmen, D. and M. Cordes (2019), *Kosten der Weiterbildung in Deutschland-Verteilung der Finanzlasten auf Unternehmen, Privatpersonen, öffentliche Hand*, https://www.fibs.eu/fileadmin/user_upload/Literatur/FiBS-Forum_061_Kosten_Weiterbildung.pdf (accessed on 15 December 2021). [12]

Eisermann, M., F. Janik and T. Kruppe (2014), "Participation in adult education: The reasons for inconsistent participation rates in different sources of data", *Zeitschrift fur Erziehungswissenschaft*, Vol. 17/3, pp. 473-495, http://dx.doi.org/10.1007/S11618-014-0561-Y. [4]

European Centre for the Development of Vocational Training (2015), "Job-related adult learning and continuing vocational training in Europe a statistical picture". [2]

Greater London Authority (2022), *Skills Roadmap for London*. [14]

Huntemann, H. et al. (2019), *Volkshochschul-Statistik – 58. Folge, Berichtsjahr 2019*, http://dx.doi.org/10.3278/85/0025w. [24]

Institute for Employment Research (2021), *Nur jeder zehnte Betrieb nutzt die Weiterbildungsförderung der Bundesagentur für Arbeit*, https://www.iab-forum.de/nur-jeder-zehnte-betrieb-nutzt-die-weiterbildungsfoerderung-der-bundesagentur-fuer-arbeit/ (accessed on 6 January 2022). [20]

KfW Research (2018), *Regionale Gesichter des Mittelstands: ein Bundeslandvergleich*, https://isb.rlp.de/fileadmin/user_upload/tt_news/2018/20180314_KfW-Mittelstandsatlas_2018.pdf (accessed on 17 December 2021). [10]

OECD (2022), *Career guidance for low-qualified workers in Germany (forthcoming)*. [15]

OECD (2021), *Continuing Education and Training in Germany*, Getting Skills Right, OECD Publishing, Paris, https://dx.doi.org/10.1787/1f552468-en. [1]

OECD (2021), *Incentives for SMEs to Invest in Skills: Lessons from European Good Practices*, Getting Skills Right, OECD Publishing, Paris, https://dx.doi.org/10.1787/1eb16dc7-en. [9]

OECD (2021), *Job retention schemes during the COVID-19 lockdown and beyond - OECD*, https://read.oecd-ilibrary.org/view/?ref=135_135415-6bardplc5q&title=Job-retention-schemes-during-the-COVID-19-lockdown-and-beyond (accessed on 4 January 2022). [17]

OECD (2021), *Social Economy - OCDE*, https://www.oecd.org/fr/cfe/leed/social-economy.htm (accessed on 14 January 2022). [28]

OECD (2021), "STOCKHOLM, Sweden - The YFI and SFX Programmes to Support Migrants - Key facts Content and mode of delivery", https://www.oecd.org/cfe/leed/OECD-Adult-Learning-Stockholm-YFIandSFX.pdf (accessed on 18 January 2022). [32]

OECD (2020), *Regional Strategies for the Social Economy - Examples from France, Spain, Sweden and Poland*, http://www.oecd.org. [29]

OECD (2019), *OECD Employment Outlook 2019: The Future of Work*, OECD Publishing, Paris, https://dx.doi.org/10.1787/9ee00155-en. [11]

Peters, J. (2020), "Dynamic agglomeration economies and learning by working in specialised regions", http://dx.doi.org/10.1093/jeg/lbz022. [6]

Senatsverwaltung für Bildung, J. (2021), *Erwachsenenbildungsgesetz vom Parlament beschlossen: Historischer Tag für Lebenslanges Lernen in Berlin*, https://www.berlin.de/sen/bjf/service/presse/pressearchiv-2021/pressemitteilung.1087304.php (accessed on 5 January 2022). [13]

Senatsverwaltung für Integration Arbeit und Soziales (2021), "Weiterbildungsprämie in der Kurzarbeit", https://www.berlin.de/sen/arbeit/weiterbildung/weiterbildungspraemie-kug/ (accessed on 4 January 2022). [18]

Senatsverwaltung für Integration Arbeit und Soziales (2020), *Beratungs-Monitor 2019*, https://www.berlin.arbeitundleben.de/cms/upload/bildung_und_digitalisierung/Beratungs-Monitor_2019.pdf (accessed on 7 January 2022). [27]

Senatsverwaltung für Integration, A. (2019), "Senatorin Breitenbach: Solo-Selbstständige arbeiten oft prekär und schlecht bezahlt", https://www.berlin.de/sen/ias/presse/pressemitteilungen/2019/pressemitteilung.842457.php (accessed on 20 December 2021). [3]

Senatsverwaltung für Integration, A. (2015), "Fachkonzept zur mobilen Bildungsberatung für geflüchtete Menschen in Berlin (MoBiBe)". [26]

Urban Innovative Actions Initiative (2021), *Urban Growth-GSIP Vantaa - Growth and Social investment Pacts for Local Companies in the City of Vantaa*, https://uia-initiative.eu/en/uia-cities/vantaa (accessed on 6 January 2022). [21]

Volkshochschule Frankfurt am Main (2020), *Praxisordner Beratung - Themen, Vorgehensweisen, Erfahrungen*, https://vhs.frankfurt.de/VHSFFM/media/Aktuelles-Teaser/Projekte/VHSffm_Bildungsberatung_Praxisordner2020.pdf (accessed on 14 December 2021). [25]

Waff (2021), *Weiterbildungsförderung für Ein-Personen-Unternehmen (EPU)*, https://www.waff.at/wp-content/uploads/2021/09/waff_infoblatt_epu_2021_lay1.pdf (accessed on 17 January 2022). [19]

Yrkesväg Värmland (2021), *Project presentation on Yrkesväg Värmland*, https://www.lansstyrelsen.se/download/18.712ccfbf17c1177f38c216c7/1634624186151/Yrkesv%C3%A4g%20V%C3%A4rmland%20English.pdf (accessed on 18 January 2022). [31]

www.ingramcontent.com/pod-product-compliance
Ingram Content Group UK Ltd.
Pitfield, Milton Keynes, MK11 3LW, UK
UKHW050413240426
12048UKWH00020B/1482

9 789264 333970